The Practical Sailor Library
Volume IV •
Do-It-Yourself
Improvement Projects

Do-It-Yourself Improvement Projects

*Upgrading for Increased Enjoyment
and Enhanced Resale Value*

Edited by Keith Lawrence

Belvoir Publications, Inc.
Riverside, Connecticut

Library of Congress Catalog Card Number: 88-071112

ISBN: 0-9613139-7-8

Printed in the United States of America
First Edition

Acknowledgments

Over the years, *The Practical Sailor* and *Better Boat* have benefit-
ted from a dedicated staff and knowledgeable contributing
editors, from the advice of numerous marine industry profes-
sions, and from the input and experience of thousands of loyal
readers. In addition to extending our thanks to all of these, we
add a special acknowledgment to the following writers for their
contribution to this volume:

Ed Adams
Ron Dwelle
Cathy Dwyer
Jim Gilbert
Greg Koveal
John R. Marples
Jack Merry
Nick Nicholson
Skip Pence
John Pazereskis
Paul E. Ring
Jerry Schindler
Matt Schultz
Jeff Spranger
Sue Weller

Contents

Introduction

The boatowner is the consummate do-it-yourselfer. For others, cruising may mean an idle stay aboard a luxury liner with a full complement of paid attendants. For most boatowners, however, cruising *means* doing it yourself. The boatowner, at the same time, is skipper and helmsman, boatswain and engineer, rigger and ship's carpenter. These do-it-yourself skills can not only save money; on occasion, these skills can save a boat—or a life.

In selecting the projects to include herein, we have endeavored to choose projects that are as interesting to read about as they are to complete. Many are simple, quick, and inexpensive, requiring little in the way of tools and mechanical skills. A few are more demanding, intended to provide a challenge for experienced craftsmen. All have one aspect in common: In addition to providing a few satisfying hours, each project will increase your enjoyment of your boat while you own it, and enhance your boat's value when you sell it.

In the winter months when your skills as a navigator and helmsman are not required, we trust that you will enjoy putting some of your other skills to work on a project or two from *Do-It-Yourself Improvement Projects*. And we trust that you will enjoy the ongoing coverage of similar improvements in *Boatbuilder*, *Better Boat* and *The Practical Sailor*, from which most of these projects have been selected.

Keith Lawrence

1

Materials and Methods

MARINE METALS

Many boatowners who routinely tackle complicated wood-working projects never give a thought to making their their own metal parts. Metalworking is similar in principle to woodworking, however, and can provide many opportunities to save money and to increase your knowledge and confidence in your boat. Often it is the welding that causes boatowners to shy away from metalworking projects. Welding is not required with many projects, and when it is, it can usually be done by a professional while still providing a savings over the cost of an off-the-shelf or a custom-fabricated part.

Buying your materials at the right price is the first way to save money on a metal part, so consider buying materials from a scrap-metal yard. Know how much you need in advance, and what alloys to look for. Go armed with a tape measure; a micrometer, caliper, or some method to measure thickness accurately; and a magnet. A hacksaw is also useful if you are looking for small pieces of aluminum stock. Most yards charge for cutting, so this will save you money. Don't try to cut stainless yourself, however, unless it is very small stock.

Most marine metal fabrication is done in stainless steel or aluminum, so we will limit our discussion to those metals. Bronze rod is often used for prop shafts and keel bolts, but it is not available in plates or sheet stock.

Stainless Steel

Stainless steel might better be called "corrosion-resisting" steel. The 300 series is best for marine use and is the only series which is non-magnetic. (That's what the magnet is for.) Check each piece for identification marks first, usually a number in the 200 to 500 range. The best alloys are 316, 321, 347, 304, 302, and 303. Alloy 303 is available only in round stock and is not weldable. All the other alloys in the 300 series are weldable.

Working stainless steel requires heavy equipment. Call sheetmetal shops to see if they can handle the thickness of metal you are using. Spray paint your sheets with an aerosol can of lacquer primer (or glue on a pattern sheet) and scratch your layout onto the surface with a straightedge. Big machinery must cut completely across the piece, so match parts of the same width end to end in strips, and cut each length separately. Make notes on the piece with a felt-tipped pen, but mark cuts and exact locations with a scribe, scratching the paint. If holes are to be punched, mark the center with a scribed "X" and the diameter with a pen next to it. Mark bends with a dashed line, and indicate the bend angle in degrees. Also indicate whether it is an "up" or "down" bend.

Cutting stainless can only be done with a shear, which is like a giant pair of hydraulic scissors that weighs several tons. It is better to punch holes in stainless steel than to drill them, although thick stainless steel can be drilled in a drill press with at least a 3/4-horsepower motor. Be prepared to sharpen drill bits frequently. Bending should be done with a "brake" over a rounded edge to avoid sharp bends. Tell the operator you want a "4T" bend. Welding requires a professional with a heli-arc welding machine. Clamp all the parts together in position, to save him time (and to save you money). Provide a wooden jig, if necessary, and a clear sketch or instructions.

Corrosion treatment of stainless steel after welding and cutting is optional. In salt water, any area that has been heated or worked will "bleed," or rust slightly but this is only a cosmetic problem. Passivation or electro-polishing will remove the cause of bleeding, and beadblasting (not sandblasting) will improve the appearance of the part. Polish the above-deck parts if you want to "shineth thy yacht to reflect the image of wealth and power" (see "Build an Inexpensive Polisher" in Chapter 2). Otherwise you can simply ease the edges and corners with a foam pad sander and bolt the part on.

Aluminum

Aluminum alloys are more difficult to classify into acceptable groups, since unlike stainless steels, their strengths vary greatly with the alloy and temper. At the risk of oversimplifying the selection, we would recommend only the 5000 and 6000 series as applicable for marine use. The preferred alloys are: 6061-T6, 6063-T4 or -T6, 5056-H18 and 5083-H32, to name a few. Generally, the larger the number following the "T" or "H," the stronger the alloy (within any specific alloy).

Working with aluminum is fairly easy, compared with stainless steel. Aluminum up to 1/4 inch in thickness can be cut on a table saw with a carbide blade, or with a metal-cutting blade on a band saw. Drilling still requires a drill press for best results, but it goes fast. The same comments about welding stainless steel apply to welding aluminum; heli-arc welding equipment should be used, and welding should only be done by a professional or an experienced amateur.

Most bends in aluminum can be made in a vise, but care should be taken to not make them too sharp—easy bends only. If stretch marks appear on the outside of the bend, examine them for cracks. Heating parts with boiling water will reduce the cracking tendency in bends, as will increasing the bend radius.

Corrosion treatment of aluminum is advised. "Hard-coat" anodize is usually very expensive, but is superior to other types. "Architectural" anodize is usually sufficient and costs much less. Aluminum winch drums are hard-coat anodized; cleats, generally are anodized by the architectural process. Colors are available (black is most common), but they are usually not color-fast, and thus fade in the sun. Anodized parts will not be completely corrosion-free as nicks and dings on the surface will start small pockets of corrosion. Aluminum hardware will last for 10 to 15 years if anodized, depending on the service and alloy.

Painting is another way to protect aluminum parts, but great care must be taken in preparing the surface; it must be absolutely clean. Simply going over the part with a sanding disc is not sufficient since bits of the abrasive cling to the aluminum and contaminants are spread from the edge of the area being cleaned and become imbedded in the surface. Aluminum can be cleaned by beadblasting or sandblasting, but this should be followed by a cleaner and conditioner, usually referred to as a "prime wash" or a "conversion coating." The conversion coating is usually a two-part treatment which cleans and etches the surface to provide the optimum adhesion of the epoxy primer and subsequent coats of paint.

* * *

The fabrication of a metal part is often easier than finding a suitable ready-made part, and just as often will prove to be the least expensive alternative. In conclusion, however, there a few cautions that should be observed when making metal parts:

• Do not use aluminum for anything underwater, or in contact with copper or bronze.

• Do not weld across any member to be put under a great deal of stress. For example, chainplate doublers should only be welded at the chainplate edges, not across the chainplate.

• Never make sharp bends in highly stressed parts. Easy bends are always best.

WOOD SELECTION
FOR IMPROVEMENT PROJECTS

For the boatowner customizing his boat, the choice of wood to use in a project can be as interesting as the design or execution of the job. Because of the overwhelming use of teak and mahogany in boatbuilding today, the opportunity to select a different wood is often overlooked.

The use of teak and mahogany is founded in practicality and tradition. Both woods are handsome, durable and workable to a superb yacht finish. For exterior uses in particular, teak is more common for a simple reason: The care of teak, compared to the demands of keeping up varnished mahogany, separates the merely industrious from the truly masochistic. Even with all the time required to keep your oiled teak looking spiffy, remember that your neighbor with varnished exterior brightwork is spending double or triple that time on his wood.

The inside of the boat is another story. While teak and mahogany are still most common, a refreshing variety of other woods can be used. Several major boatbuilders have been experimenting with different varieties below—a trend which we encourage. Perhaps the most important factor in the choice is that the wood fit in appropriately. This requirement does not limit the choice to woods that are already in the boat, but it certainly includes them.

The choice of a species of wood is a subjective call. The color, grain and traditional uses of a particular wood will speak to one craftsman and his fellow in different ways. Traditional woods, for example, vary according to region (white cedar is common in the eastern U.S., western red cedar on the Pacific Coast, for example). A contrasting wood can lend warmth, lightness and elegance to the interior, but the varieties should be limited in number to prevent the appearance of confusion and clutter.

Less subjective is whether a wood has the appropriate characteristics to do a particular job. Holly splines are used in teak cabin soles for the contrasting light color and because it does not turn black when exposed to water. Ash turns black when exposed to water, so it should be used only in relatively dry locations and should always be varnished. Cedar is too soft for heavy wear applications, but serves well for ceilings. Hardwoods hold fastening better than soft, but softer woods often glue better. The weight, durability, hardness, strength, and workability of the wood should all be taken into account in matching the wood to its work.

Finally, there are the two other factors which control the choice: cost and availability. Some exotic woods which are highly desirable are too expensive to be worth the cost, or are simply unavailable in this country. In some cases, the local wood is the best choice simply because of its availability. If you are doing extensive refurbishing, it may be worth a special order of the wood of your choice, but since transportation comprises a large part of lumber costs, it is still worth checking out the regionally grown species.

When purchasing wood, keep in mind that it has almost certainly been kiln-dried, which may have lowered its moisture content to below ten percent. The appropriate range for woodworking is generally regarded as around 15 percent. Time for seasoning should be built in to your work schedule to avoid large changes in the size and shape of the wood, particularly when large or long pieces are used in tight spaces.

A summary of some of the readily available woods for boatbuilding use follows. This list is by no means exhaustive, but it should cover most applications.

Teak

A dark and heavy wood of golden brown hue, teak is moderately hard and very resistant to decay. Although fairly easy to work, it splits easily and requires care to prevent unwanted fractures, particularly when drilling for fasteners. Because of a high silica content in the wood, tools dull quickly and carbide cutting blades are recommended. Its natural oiliness, which contributes to its rot resistance, also causes it to clog sandpaper quickly and can cause problems in gluing. It should be degreased with a solvent before gluing.

Teak is the overwhelming choice for exterior applications. It is durable and perhaps most important, can be recovered from a weathered state with relative ease. It should be oiled or varnished to prevent warping and checking which can result from neglect. With the exception of spars, teak is suitable for any exterior use.

Down below, teak is best for cabin soles and high-wear applications and can be finished with a teak sealer or oil rather than varnished, in the interest of reducing maintenance. High demand and export restrictions have made teak comparatively expensive, running $7 to $10 a board foot.

Iroko

Iroko ("African teak") resembles true Far Eastern teak in appearance, and is often used as a substitute for the real thing. Iroko is highly rot resistant and durable, and will take a fine varnish finish, although due to its coarser grain structure it is more difficult to work with than teak. Iroko is somewhat less expensive than teak, but is generally considered to be less satisfactory when left bare in exterior applications.

Mahogany

A medium to dark reddish color characterizes this wood of medium weight and hardness, although color varies from pink to dark brown. Honduras mahogany is preferable to African mahogany because the latter often has a highly figured, unruly grain which is difficult to plane smooth.

When used above decks, mahogany is elegant in appearance, but time-consuming to maintain. It must be varnished to prevent darkening from exposure, and usually looks best if stained to produce a uniform color. Darkened wood can be bleached, but not always completely.

In general, the mahoganies work easily and glue well. The price varies with quality but is generally in the moderate range.

Lauan

Often called "Philippine mahogany," lauan is actually a member of the cedar family. It is available in light and dark red varieties, with the lighter type being softer and less durable than the dark. The darker lauan is generally comparable to Honduras and African mahoganies for most uses, although when varnished, it lacks the rich grain texture of the true mahoganies.

Most of the lauan imported into this country is in the form of plywood. Lauan plywood is used extensively in small boat construction where its moderate rot resistance is usually enhanced by an epoxy coating or FRP sheathing. Lauan plywood is preferred over Douglas fir by some builders for bulkheads and interior joinerwork in larger vessels, due to the fact that it takes a fine painted finish. Lauan lumber and plywood are in the low to moderate cost range.

Butternut

A native American wood of light color and light weight, butternut is soft, works easily, and must be varnished to protect its color and surface. It should be used in relatively protected locations, due to its softness. Butternut is commonly used for joinerwork and ceilings, and is particularly attractive when trimmed with mahogany. A traditional wood in some of the better American yacht yards, butternut is not readily available outside the northeastern U.S.

American Ash

Light in color, heavy in weight, ash is native to the eastern United States. It has a very hard surface, but works well with sharp tools and splits less readily than oak. Because it turns black if left exposed, it must be varnished. It is suitable for either ceiling or trim, but its weight should be considered where large amounts might be required. Due to its light color and interesting grain texture, ash veneer plywood is becoming increasingly popular for use in yacht interiors.

White Cedar

Very light in color and weight, white cedar is soft, dents easily, but is easy to work and glue. It is often used as a planking material and occasionally for joinerwork and ceilings. It is likely to be knotty, so there is a fair amount of waste, which must be anticipated when ordering stock. As it will turn gray quickly if left exposed, it must be painted or varnished. White cedar is slightly aromatic and relatively inexpensive.

Western Red Cedar

Native to the northwestern United States, red cedar is generally comparable to white cedar, except for its darker reddish color, greater aroma, and clearer grain. It is light, strong, resistant to rot, and offers excellent paint and glue adhesion. These qualities, along with its relatively low cost and excellent bending properties, have helped to make western red cedar the material of choice for hull and deck construction in cold-molded veneer.

Redwood

Native to California, redwood's characteristics are similar to red cedar. It varies in color from cherry to dark mahogany with a narrow white sapwood. Light in weight and moderately hard, it works easily and glues well, with high natural resistance to decay. It can be very attractive varnished, and is appropriate for cabinetwork and paneling.

White Pine

Very light in color and weight, white pine is moderately soft and works easily. Much of what is sold as "white pine" in the eastern U.S. is actually one of several species of eastern spruce. Neither wood is easy to find in long, clear lengths; but if carefully selected and protected from rot, either can serve well for decking, ceiling, and general joinerwork. Because both pine and spruce are commonly employed for non-marine applications, the lesser grades are low in cost and readily available.

Southern Yellow Pine

The various southern pines (longleaf, slash, loblolly) that are collectively referred to as yellow pine or pitch pine have long been a favorite of boatbuilders in the southeastern states. Its decay resistance, ability to hold fasteners, and availability in long, clear lengths makes it ideal for planking and decking. For heavy structural members, yellow pine is often substituted for white oak. For lighter structural members such as stringers, clamps, and chine logs, it is an acceptable, if somewhat heavier, substitute for Douglas fir.

Although yellow pine works easily and accepts paints, varnishes, and adhesives with little difficulty, it lacks the aesthetic appeal of some of the other light-colored woods such as ash, birch, butternut, and white oak when used for bright-finished joinerwork. It is readily available at relatively low cost in the eastern United States.

Douglas Fir

Douglas fir is a member of the pine family, abundant in the northwestern U.S. and Canada, and probably the single most important forest products produced in the western hemisphere. There are certainly many species that surpass Douglas fir in one characteristic or another. Probably none, however, when cost is considered, can match its combination of desirable qualities for marine use or in the building trades. Like yellow pine, Douglas fir cannot compare to the natural beauty of some of the other light-colored hardwoods for joinerwork and trim applications. Still (with the possible exception of Douglas fir plywood), it is not unattractive when finished bright.

Sitka Spruce

While it does require care to prevent decay, Sitka spruce has long been the favorite for spars, stringers, and other applications where a high strength-to-weight ratio is required. It is light in weight and in color, working easily with sharp hand and power tools. Long, clear lengths are easier to obtain on the West Coast, being closer to the source (the west coast of Canada to Alaska). Usually, it is only available on special order in the eastern U.S., and then only at a premium price.

Yellow Birch

Birch is a relatively heavy, moderately hard wood that varies in color from bluish white sapwood to light, pinkish orange heartwood. It is an excellent choice for joinerwork as it works and glues easily, and remains relatively stable dimensionally. The general availability of low-cost birch veneer plywood also helps to make birch a good choice for interior finishing projects. Birch is not rot resistant and thus needs protection from moisture. It has an attractive appearance when finished bright, but any clear coating should contain an ultraviolet filter (even when used belowdecks); otherwise, birch tends to turn yellow-orange within a short period of time.

White Oak

The mighty *Quercus alba* is the shipbuilding timber against which all others have been judged for many centuries. Although modern fasteners, adhesives, and construction methods have reduced the demand for it, unseasoned white oak is still required when steam bending is necessary; and a rubrail of varnished white oak, capped with a bronze band, is still the hallmark of a serious cruising vessel.

Despite its reputation as being tough and stringy, when properly seasoned, white oak is an easily worked wood for joinerwork and interior trim. It is often combined with oak veneer plywood to produce light, elegant interior spaces.

Red Oak

Except for its lower resistance to decay, red oak has all the excellent qualities and properties of white oak. It is also an easily worked lumber, suitable for structural applications as well as fine cabinetwork and joinery. Like white oak, it also requires care in the choice of fastening and finishing techniques to avoid staining from moisture and corroded fasteners.

SELECTING PLYWOOD FOR MARINE USE

Even though the revolution in fiberglass construction has eclipsed the traditional wooden construction methods, plywood continues to be a staple of the boatbuilding industry. Highly regarded for its durability and dimensional stability, plywood is becoming increasingly popular for hull construction; and plywood is now the standard construction material for bulkheads, interior components, hatch covers and numerous other items—even on boats built of fiberglass, steel, and aluminum.

As an engineered product for which design stresses and section properties have been calculated and published, softwood plywood offers numerous advantages as a construction material. By cross-laminating layers of wood veneer, plywood provides an excellent strength-to-weight ratio, and exhibits superior stiffness along both the length and width of the panel. Plywood improves on wood's well-known ability to absorb impact shocks, and delivers secure fastener-holding ability. The cross-lamination principle also yields excellent dimensional stability, and resistance to warping or buckling in the plane of the panel. While solid timber tends to shrink more across the grain than along the grain with changes in moisture content, in plywood, the tendency of individual veneers to swell or shrink is greatly restricted by the relative longitudinal stability of the adjacent plies.

Plywood is inexpensive, readily available, and easily worked. It can be cut, drilled, routed, jointed, glued, fastened and finished with ordinary tools and basic skills. It can also be bent to form curved surfaces without loss of strength; an important consideration when selecting materials for new boat construction, repairs and upgrading projects.

Softwood plywood is produced in three basic exposure durability classifications. Exterior-type panels are made with a fully waterproof glue, and are designed for applications subject to continuous exposure to the weather or moisture. Panels marked "Exposure 1" are made with the same exterior phenolic resin adhesive used in exterior-grade panels and are highly resistant to moisture. However, because the lower grade of veneer permitted in the manufacture of exposure-1 panels may affect glueline performance, only exterior-grade panels should be used for permanent exposure to moisture. Interior panels lacking additional glueline information in their trademarks are usually manufactured with interior glue and are intended for interior applications only.

Several grades of softwood plywood lend themselves to boat applications, with one grade—*marine*, as the name suggests—especially well suited to the task. Although "U.S. Product Standard PS 1-83 for Construction and Industrial Plywood" permits over 70 species of wood for the manufacture of softwood plywood, marine grade is manufactured in the U.S. only with Douglas fir or western larch, and only in exterior type. It has solid jointed cores and highly restrictive limitations on core gaps and face repairs. Marine plywood is ideal for boat hulls and other applications where bending is involved, although exterior plywood is usually quite suitable for interior joinerwork. Marine plywood is available in many thicknesses including 1/4, 3/8, 1/2, 5/8, 3/4, and one inch. Although it is sometimes difficult to locate at your local building material retailer, marine-grade plywood is well worth the boatbuilder's search, particularly if it is to be used for hull construction.

Marine plywood is one of several grades of plywood that are classified as "sanded." Other sanded grades include A-A, A-B, A-C, A-D, B-B, B-C and B-D. The letters denote the grade of the face and back veneers. A is the highest grade, D the lowest. There also exists a premium N-grade veneer panel available only by special order. A-C and B-C are made only in exterior grade; A-A, A-B, and B-C in all three exposure durability classifications; and A-D and B-D in exposure 1 and interior grade only. Sanded panel thicknesses range from 1/4 to 3/4 inch.

Sanded trademarks also include a group number denoting

the species group from which the face and back veneers are made. There are five species groups. Group 1 species are the strongest and stiffest, group 2 the next highest in strength, and so on. Most of the plywood manufactured today is made from group-1 species. However, it should be noted that when face and back veneers are from different species, the higher group number is normally used.

High and medium-density overlay plywood (HDO and MDO) are two additional grades of special interest to do-it-yourselfers. These are manufactured with a hard resin-treated fiber overlay, bonded under heat and pressure to one or both sides of the panel. The overlay provides an extremely durable and abrasion-resistant surface. Overlaid panels are made only in exterior grade and are available from some manufacturers with a skid-resistant, screen-grid surface.

Fir plywood has one distinct disadvantage: No matter how well you seal the surface, it tends to check over time. These checks are tiny surface cracks which do not affect the wood structurally, but are difficult to hide with paint. Medium-density overlay plywood, on the other hand, provides an ideal base for paint finishes, and is excellent for interior joinery projects as well as hull and deck planking.

Imported Plywood

Of the foreign-made plywoods, lauan marine plywood is popular with boatbuilders, and for good reason. Lauan, usually called Philippine mahogany, comes from huge trees that are largely free of knots and other flaws. Although most lauan plywood is relatively lifeless and dull in color, it can be stained with mahogany stain and varnished for a presentable surface.

The face plies of better grades of lauan ply are unlikely to have patches. Lauan makes excellent inner plies because there are rarely any knots to be patched. Rot resistance is comparable to Douglas fir plywood.

Lauan is usually used for the core plies of plywood faced with other veneers. So-called teak marine plywood is only faced with teak; usually, the interior plies are lauan.

Unfortunately, not all lauan plywood is marine grade. Tremendous quantities of lauan plywood are imported from the Far

East for the home construction trade, particularly for carpet and tile underlayment. Unless it is specified as marine grade (and the standard to which it is built is marked on the plywood), you can assume that a piece of lauan plywood is exterior grade rather than marine.

The best lauan plywood is made to British Standard 1088 WBP, which is a waterproof and boilproof marine plywood. The edge of each piece of high-grade ply will be stamped with both the name of the manufacturer and the standard to which the plywood is made.

There are a variety of other mahoganies and pseudo-mahoganies made into plywood, including khaya, utile, sapele, and okume, but unless these other varieties have specific properties in which you are interested, they offer no particular advantage for most interior work. The color and texture of all species will vary from sheet to sheet, so don't count on matching grain or color with what is already in your boat.

Determining Plywood Quality

To some extent, the number of plies in the sheet is as much a determinant of quality as the grade and type of veneer. Plywood that consists of two surface veneers plus a thick, single core, is called "lumber-core" plywood. It is suitable only for nonstructural applications such as cabinet doors and drawer fronts.

Half-inch structural plywood should be made up of at least five, but preferably seven laminations. the better grades of 3/4-inch ply will be made up of nine to 13 layers, although seven plies are normal for lower priced marine lauan. More layers mean greater strength and stiffness.

Even if you have only a few projects in mind, it will pay you to go to the trouble to buy a good grade of plywood for your boat. The cost is small relative to the amount of time you spend on any project. At the same time, it is possible to go overboard. It does not make sense, for example, to use teak-veneered plywood for shelves, unless the other shelves in your boat are also made of teak plywood. Nor is it necessary to use a very high-grade marine plywood such as Bruynzeel, unless the other wood on your boat is of the same quality. Remember, whatever you do to your boat should match the quality and style of what is already there. If you put in materials that are better than what was put in by the builder, the lesser work will look shabby by comparison.

Working with Plywood

The best plywood in the world will not last if not treated properly, beginning from the time you buy it. Plywood should be stored lying flat, but should not be placed directly on a concrete floor. Use 2x4s or other lumber—all of the same thickness—to raise the plywood off the ground. Obviously, store it under cover, preferably inside. Never store plywood on edge; it will gradually bend.

Plywood can be cut with a table saw, bandsaw, hand-held circular saw, saber saw, or a plain old handsaw. Whatever tool you use, make sure you have the right blade, one designed for a finish cut in wood. (Leave your eight-point rip saw hanging on the wall when cutting plywood.)

Plywood tends to splinter badly when cut across the grain of the surface plies. This tearout can be greatly reduced by taping the surface of the sheet with masking tape before cutting. Strike the cutting line on the surface for reference, tape over it with masking tape, then restrike the line on the masking tape. Likewise, taping corners and edges while handling will reduce the chances of damage.

You can true up and fit the edges of plywood with a sharp block plane, a jack plane, or even a rasp. Remember, however, that grain tearout is a real danger. Keep the edges or sides of the plywood taped, and keep your tools extremely sharp. The brittle glue used to make the plywood will quickly dull your tools.

When installing plywood, all surfaces, including the edges, should be sealed with paint, varnish, or resin, depending on the application. Plywood edges should not be left exposed, except in lightweight construction using high-grade plywood. When making shelves without fiddles, a narrow piece of solid lumber matching the other solid wood in the interior can be glued and nailed to the exposed edges, whether they are to be painted or varnished. No matter how many coats of paint you put on a raw edge of plywood, the end grain of the core plies will show.

In our experience, glued-on veneers used to hide the edge grain have a limited lifespan. They get chipped off, or the glue eventually lets go and they peel off. A piece of solid lumber, 1/4 inch thick, glued to the edge of a piece of plywood with epoxy resin is there for keeps. Alternatively, fiddles on shelves can simply overlap the edge, hiding the end grain.

Never leave plywood unfinished. We have seen many boats with teak plywood companionway dropboards, which are often left unvarnished. The plywood may be waterproof, and the teak surface veneer will not rot, but the lauan core eventually will. If you have teak plywood dropboards, a good project is to glue solid teak to the exposed plywood edge grain. Even so, it is best to varnish plywood dropboards.

*   *   *

Plywood is a wonderfully versatile material. Its laminated construction makes it a natural companion to fiberglass for boat construction, and particularly suited for many projects both above and belowdecks.

Additional information about softwood plywood for marine applications is available from the American Plywood Association (P. O. Box 11700; Tacoma, Washington 98411).

CHOOSING A WATERPROOF ADHESIVE

Almost from the dawn of man, we have used our ingenuity to make things stick together. In fact, whether used in the making of tools or other necessities, joining different materials may have been the first example of technology. Archaeologists have removed statues from Babylonian temples—statues with eyeballs glued to their sockets with bituminous cements that held fast for 6,000 years. Paintings found in tombs near the ancient Egyptian city of Thebes dating back about 3400 years depict a gluing operation for veneering. Egyptian mummies were wrapped in linens saturated with resins and waxy gums to protect both the body and the wrappings from deterioration—probably the first example of sheathing, while Roman ships were caulked with pine tar and beeswax.

Most of the primitive adhesives came from the sap, leaves, bark, and roots of trees; and from the hides, hooves, and bones of animals. Some adhesives of this type are still in use today. It was the scientific explosion in the second quarter of this century, however, that provided us with synthetic materials of remarkable strength, uniformity, and reliability. From filtertip cigarettes, which use over a dozen adhesives in their manufacture, to the B-58 delta-wing aircraft which utilizes structural adhesives to the exclusion of rivets, modern adhesive technology has come a long way.

It is helpful in considering adhesives to recognize that they posses a remarkably unique property—the have no identity by themselves. They are adhesives only to the extent that they bond to some other material or materials. The end-product, a structural element, should be looked upon as a system consisting of two surfaces joined by an adhesive. These structual elements, or joints, may have a variety of configurations, but all joints are variations of four basic types, as defined by the manner in which they are stressed. These stresses are shear, tension, cleavage, and peel. Since the nature of the stress in a joint has a great influence on the adhesive characteristics required to function most effectively in that configuration, before we talk much about adhesives we ought to consider the stresses which must be withstood. The four basic stress modes are explained below and illustrated in **Figure 1-1**.

1. SHEAR. Force is exerted across the adhesive bond. The bonded surfaces are being forced to slide over each other. All of the adhesive contributes to bond strength.

2. TENSILE. Force is exerted at right angles to the adhesive equally over the entire joint. All of the adhesive contributes to bond strength.

3. CLEAVAGE. Force is concentrated at one edge of the joint and exerts a prying force on the bond. The other edge of the joint is theoretically under zero stress. Only a portion of the adhesive resists load.

4. PEEL. One surface must be flexible. Stress is concentrated along a thin line at the edge of the bond where separation occurs. A very small portion of the adhesive carries all the peeling force.

Most adhesives perform better when the primary stress is shear or tensile. However, in most applications a combination of stresses is involved. For best performance the entire bond area should carry the bulk of the stress.

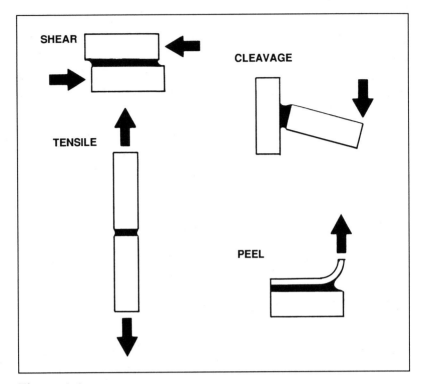

Figure 1-1.

In addition to the stress mode, other factors influence the selection of an adhesive. Environmental exposure is an important consideration; moisture, temperature extremes, impact, vibration, chemical contact, dimensional changes, and biological attack all impose added requirements on the adhesive.

Next, application requirements or process limitations must be examined. Is the adhesive easy to use? Are special tools required? How much working time is needed? What is the range of application and curing temperatures? How critical is the condition and fitting of the surfaces? Is clamping pressure important to the ultimate strength of the bond? Can dissimilar materials be bonded?

Finally, the nature of the cured product is of concern. Is color important or will staining detract from the finished product? Will the adhesive be compatible with materials applied later?

What is the anticipated life of the adhesive under the expected service conditions?

Having outlined some of the requirements that an effective adhesive must meet, we can now open the chemist's cupboard and see what he has to offer. Most home-built boats and projects aboard a boat are made of wood—Mother Nature's own reinforced plastic. Thus, most of the adhesives we find are primarily intended for bonding wood; and since boats are usually used in the water, the adhesives are waterproof.

Three major types of waterproof adhesives are available today, and we identify them by their approximate chemical names: resorcinol, ureaformaldehyde, and epoxy. Although they are not considered to be "glues," several other adhesive sealants are available (silicone, polysulfide, polyurethane), but we will deal with them separately later in this chapter.

Resorcinol Adhesives

Having already noted some of the characteristics that these adhesives have in common, let us now consider how they differ. Resorcinol adhesives have been available for over 25 years. The adhesive is generally supplied as a powder which is mixed with a specified quantity of water immediately prior to use (two-part resorcinol comes as a liquid resin and a powdered hardener). After mixing, resorcinol remains semi-fluid for periods ranging from 20 minutes to 2 hours, depending on the type, and is easily applied with a brush, spatula, or a stick. Most manufacturers recommend that the temperature of the workroom, the adhesive, and the surfaces to be bonded should not be lower than 70 degrees F during application and cure.

Resorcinol should not be used if the wood has a moisture content above 15 per cent. It need be applied to only one of the two mating surfaces, and care must be taken to avoid disturbing the joint after 20-30 minutes following clamping. The most critical characteristics of resorcinol are its dependence on glue line thickness and clamping pressure. In its *Bulletin 400*, U.S. Plywood Corporation states: "...for best results, sufficient pressure to reduce the glue line to a thickness of 0.005 is required. Thicker glue lines will result in an inferior bond...but high pressure should not be substituted for poor fitting joints."

When relatively thin and flexible wood, such as plywood, is fastened down by screws, there may not be adequate pressure except near the screws. With annular nails rather than screws, the situation is more serious since one cannot achieve nearly as much pressure, particularly when there is tension at the joint which is to be pulled together.

When hardened, resorcinol tends to be brittle and inelastic, limiting its use to relatively rigid surfaces where peel and cleavage forces are negligible and vibration and impact unlikely. Care must be taken to avoid smears and runs with resorcinol as it produces dark stains on most timbers. In laminated structures which will be exposed to view, the dark color of the glue line may also be objectionable. We should also note that resorcinol does not produce reliable joints with oak, especially if subjected to repeated wetting and drying.

All this does not mean that sound boats and first-class upgrading projects cannot be built with resorcinol adhesives, but it does point out that care is needed if one is to avoid joints of substandard strength.

Urea Adhesives

Urea adhesives are available as both one-part and two-part systems. The one-part system is prepared by mixing with water, much the same as resorcinol. The two-part types are supplied as separate resin and hardener components. The resin may be a liquid to be used as is, or a powder which is mixed with water prior to use. (Perhaps the best known of this type is Aerolite 300 and 306.) The two-part ureas are used in a manner that many might consider unique. Instead of mixing the resin and hardener together as is done with polyester and epoxy resins, you apply the resin to one of the surfaces and the hardener to the other. When the surfaces are brought together, the curing reaction begins, and proceeds at a rate dependent on the temperature of the surfaces; the warmer it is the faster the adhesive cures. Urea-type adhesives cure rather slowly below 50-55 degrees F, and may fail completely if the surfaces are below 45 degrees.

The wood should be clean, dust-free, and dry. Plywood should be roughened slightly with sandpaper if it appears to have a glaze from the heated presses used in its manufacture. Fit and clamping pressure are not nearly as critical as for resorcinol; glue lines may be as thick as 1/32 inch, and clamping pressure need be no greater than that required to bring the surfaces together. As we mentioned, curing begins upon contact, and after about 20 minutes at 70 degrees F, the adhesive has substantially solidified (although not fully cured) to the extent that the joint may not be closed further. In warmer weather, gelation is even more rapid, sometimes necessitating fast work and a helper or two.

Cured ureas are light straw-colored to transparent and will not produce unsightly stains. Adhesive squeezed out of joints can be cleaned up with a damp cloth if not permitted to cure too long. When using two-part ureas it is mandatory that panels be marked on the interior before gluing in order to identify mating surfaces for proper application of resin and hardener. It is particularly important not to omit the hardener or allow it to dry out before mating the surfaces, as the resin portion will merely dry (as opposed to curing) in a few hours and be almost indistinguishable from properly cured resin (except that it will later dissolve in water).

Epoxy Adhesives

Epoxy adhesives come more close to being "universal" adhesives than any other. They adhere with equal tenacity to wood, fiberglass, concrete, and most metals. Virtually all room-temperature-curing epoxy adhesives come as two-part kits consisting of a separate resin and hardener. The variety-store blister pack epoxies should be avoided for several reasons. First of all, they are made to sell at a low price and may be heavily laced with filler, diluents, and extenders, all of which may contribute to brittleness and poor long-term water-resistance. Second, their uniformity varies considerably and users frequently do not get predictable results. Third, the buyer actually ends up paying more per ounce for the twin-tube kits than he would for superior epoxies packaged in pints, quarts, and gallons. Finally, an epoxy to be used for structural purposes should be acknowledged by the seller to be intended for that type of service.

Marine epoxy adhesives are supplied in kits consisting of two bottles of rather viscous liquids designated A (resin) and B (hardener). These are mixed in various ratios such as 4:1, 5:1, or in equal amount by volume in the case of Chem-Tech's T-88 epoxy. At 70 degrees F, the user has about 45 minutes to apply the adhesive if he has mixed a total of eight ounces or less. Larger quantities have a shorter pot life, while smaller volumes have a longer one. This is due to the fact that when resin and hardener are mixed, a chemical reaction begins (polymerization), and this reaction produces heat. The larger the mass of adhesive, the greater the amount of heat, the faster the reaction goes, generating more heat, and so on. When the adhesive is squeezed out in a thin layer between two relatively massive surfaces, the polymerization reaction, of course, continues; except now the heat generated is absorbed by the surfaces and does not serve to accelerate the cure. That is why a few ounces of adhesive in a cup may gel in an hour or less, while the same amount of adhesive between two surfaces will remain workable for several hours.

Epoxy is easily applied with a flat stick, and because resin and hardener are mixed in the same cup, it need only be applied to one of the mating surfaces. Wood surfaces should be clean and dust-free, although oily woods like teak should first be wiped with lacquer thinner for best results. Some epoxy adhesives may be applied to damp surfaces, which is helpful in making laminated curved structures where soaking or steaming is required.

Fit and clamping pressure do not present any problems since epoxies are truly gap-filling and require only sufficient pressure to hold the surfaces together. Bonds have been made to wood where the glue line exceeded 1/16 inch and testing shows that the joint will always fail in the wood. Where gaps are large, a thickening powder can be used to keep the epoxy from running out of the joint.

Epoxy will remain workable in a joint for two hours or more, allowing for more leisurely clamping or fastening of large panels without concern that the joints may not fully close. Squeezed-out adhesive may be removed with a stick before it fully hardens, and any final traces will come off with lacquer thinner which can also be used to clean up tools. (Solvents must never be used to clean the hands as they tend to remove protective skin oils and may actually intensify skin irritation.) Once the epoxy has hardened, virtually no solvent will dissolve it and mechanical removal must be used. Epoxy is clear or light amber in color, will not discolor wood, and becomes invisible when varnished.

Often, one of the problems with projects around a boat is temperature. Urea adhesives cannot be used below about 50 degrees F, while resorcinol gets risky below 65 degrees. Some epoxies, on the other hand, can be applied and will cure clear down to 35 degrees F, although at this low temperature hardening may take a week.

At more moderate temperatures, most epoxies will harden in 6 to 8 hours and reach full strength after about a day. The cured adhesive is slightly resilient and withstands vibration, impact, and cleavage; while being resistant to fungus, rot, and virtually all fuels and chemicals likely to be found around a boat.

A final comment should be made regarding allergic reactions to epoxy resins and curing agents. While most resin manufacturers take care to avoid those compounds which are strong irritants, there will always be a few people who will have or may develop an allergy to epoxies. The best approach is prevention. Avoid skin contact and excessive inhalation of vapors. Wear disposable latex gloves, and work in an area with reasonable ventilation. If you should get epoxy on the skin, clean up promptly with an appropriate skin cleanser or soap and water. Never use acetone or other solvents on the skin. Note that these precautions apply only to uncured epoxy materials; once the adhesive has hardened it becomes quite inert.

THE PROPER FASTENER

Do you remember Richard III's lament about losing a battle for lack of a nail? By contrast, use a nail in a fiberglass boat and it is likely that the boat will be lost. Nails, as well as wood screws, have few applications on a modern boat. The reason is simple: Almost any fastener will do a better job than either.

The most practical fastener material is stainless steel. Stainless steel is strong, corrosion-resistant, and galvanically the most passive of fastener materials with the exception of bronze. Best of all, stainless steel fasteners are commonly available, even in areas where an anchor is regarded as an odd example of free-form sculpture.

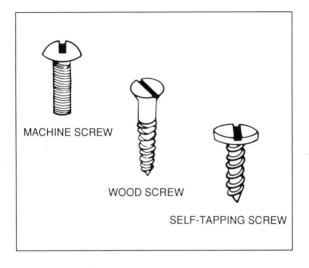

MACHINE SCREW

WOOD SCREW

SELF-TAPPING SCREW

The three most common types of fastener on the modern boat have mutually exclusive uses. It is rare that one can be substituted for another.

Let's take a close look at the choice of fasteners available to the do-it-yourself boatowner:

Screws

There is almost nothing aboard a boat that can't be fastened with the self-tapping screw (also called a sheetmetal screw). Self-tapping screws are, of course, ideal for screwing into thin, hard metals or even moderately thick soft metal such as aluminum. All it takes is a pilot hole drilled to the optimum diameter.

Self-tapping screws work almost as well in most woods as they do in metal. They come in a variety of head configurations in sizes up to #14, and in lengths from 1/4 inch to 3 inches. Just like a wood screw, a self-tapper can be countersunk and bunged, or set with the head flush.

Where self-tapping screws truly excel is in fastening into fiberglass laminates, whether cored or solid. They should be used to carry light loads only, however; they are not a substitute for bolts for heavier loads. As with any screw, the strength of the fastening itself is generally greater than its holding power (it will pull out before it will break off). As a rule of thumb, the laminate into which the screw is driven should be at least equal in thickness to the diameter of the screw.

For all their virtues, self-tapping screws do have some notable limitations and drawbacks. The number of times they can

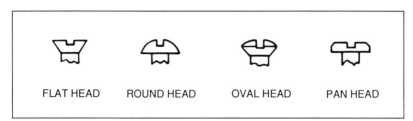

FLAT HEAD   ROUND HEAD   OVAL HEAD   PAN HEAD

The four most common and useful screw-head configurations. Round-head and pan-head fasteners are generally used in applications where the screw head will stand proud, while flat-head and oval-head screws are usually countersunk to set flush with the surface.

be removed and redriven is finite; sooner or later they wear out the hole, diminishing their holding power. Holding power is also reduced if the pilot hole is oversized, and they may be impossible to drive if the pilot hole is undersized. Remember too that the holding power of the screw is no greater than the strength of the material into which it is driven. Soft woods, thin laminates, and thin metals cannot carry much of a load.

Conventional wood screws are superior for fastening wood joinerwork, but they should never be used to fasten into fiberglass laminates.

Bolts

For heavier loads, for pulling two surfaces together, and for fastenings that may be repetitively tightened and loosened, bolts are the answer. These functions are in direct contrast to those that screws perform best. Machine screws come with flat, round, and oval heads, all slotted for use with a screwdriver. Other bolts are available with hexagonal and square heads for use with a wrench; recessed (socket) heads for Allen wrenches; and rounded, carriage heads. Nuts for use with these bolts are hexagonal, square, wing (for hand tightening), jam (self-locking, also called aircraft nuts), and cap (acorn). All are capable of taking a variety of washers underneath. Machine screws are often used in heavier metal without a nut by drilling and tapping the hole. (To be used in this manner, the metal should be at least as thick as the diameter of the bolt.)

Nuts are intended to be tightened against a washer. The

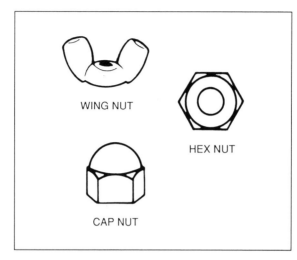

The three most common types of nuts; wing, hex, and cap; also have specialized applications.

washer not only spreads the load on the lower surface of the material being bolted, but prevents the nut from cutting into that surface. As many applications aboard a boat involve heavy localized loading—more load than a washer alone can handle—bolts may need a hard backing block of aluminum or fiberglass in addition to a washer to better spread that load. A good sealant should always be used with through-bolts in a hull or deck, as the bolt holes provide passageways for water.

Rivets

Pop-Rivet is a brand name, but rightly or wrongly, the term is becoming generic for the type of blind fastener that expands when the center pin (mandrel) is extracted and broken off. Such rivets are commonly used in applications that would call for a bolt, but where location prevents turning on a nut (in attaching mast fittings, for example). Since pop rivets are also quicker to install, they are frequently used instead of bolts in production applications (such as the hull-to-deck joints on smaller and cheaper boats).

Pop-rivets are available in both aluminum and stainless steel, with the stainless steel ones use for heavier loads. The center pin is pulled, expanding the body of the rivet, until the pin breaks ("pops"). They may be set up with either a hand tool or a hydraulic tool. A word of warning: Squeezing the hand tool is a macho exercise, difficult for the aluminum rivets, herculean for the stainless steel.

Removing rivets entails drilling them out, a job that must be done carefully to prevent enlarging the holes in which replacement rivets must fit. In removing rivets (for stripping a mast for painting, for instance), you may want to plan from the outset to use the next larger diameter when you replace the rivets.

* * *

Fasteners bought one by one, or even a dozen at a time, are outrageously priced. Bought individually, or in a blister pack of five or six, a one-inch, #10 sheetmetal screw will cost about 15 cents. Bought in bulk, typically 100 to a box, they run closer to 5 cents apiece. At $4 a box, the same money that buys three dozen individual screws will buy a box of a hundred. If you don't want to pass on the extra screws as part of your estate, surprise your fellow sailors with the gift of a handful.

And finally, keep in mind that a well found yacht does not need an infinite variety of fastener sizes and types. A typical 35-footer can be built with just a few basic fasteners: 3/16-inch and 1/4-inch flathead machine screws in two or three different lengths, a box or two of #8 and #10 self-tapping screws in 3/4 and 1-1/4 inch lengths, and a couple boxes of #8 wood screws for the joiner work. Where the underside of a bolt or screw is hidden, the excess length makes no difference except to a racing sailor for whom any extra weight is a cause for fantods. Of course, don't leave the excess length exposed where it can cause an injury or snag a sail.

SYNTHETIC RUBBER-BASED ADHESIVE SEALANTS

Years ago, no matter what sort of a seam-sealing or bedding operation you had in mind, you picked up a putty knife and a can of oil-based bedding compound. Oil-based compounds rarely failed due to problems caused by incompatibility with other boatbuilding materials; they always failed within a few years, however, due to drying, cracking, and lack of adhesion.

Over the past decade, oil-based bedding compounds have all but disappeared from the shelves of marine hardware stores and ship chandleries. They have been supplanted by synthetic rubber adhesive sealants. The synthetic rubber compounds typically last for ten to twenty years or more. Nevertheless, a tube of adhesive sealant must be chosen much more carefully than a can of bedding compound; the various polymers exhibit vastly different properties, and frequently fail due to incompatibility with other materials.

When we first began to examine these newer polymers, we had hoped to identify a single compound that would be suitable for all bedding and sealing uses, both above and below the waterline. What we discovered was that even though all types of sealants are described with words such as "waterproof," "permanent," "flexible," and "safe for use above and below the waterline"; they are not identical or interchangeable. The use of each type of polymer is, in at least one sense, a compromise, and each has advantages offset by disadvantages.

Although there are various proprietary compounds (often mixtures of two or more polymers) that exhibit various combinations of characteristics, the choice of an adhesive sealant usually comes down to one of "the big three": the silicones, the polysulfides, and the polyurethanes. Its no accident that these are the most common and most widely recommended marine adhesive sealants; with one of them, virtually any bedding and sealing problem can be solved.

Of the three major categories of synthetic rubbers, all have applications aboard boats built of metal and wood, as well as those built of fiberglass. We must admit, however, that it is easier to choose a compound for use on a fiberglass boat, simply because there are fewer variables associated with fiberglass surfaces. On wood and metal boats, surface preparation plays a much larger role in the performance of an adhesive sealant. There are also variables introduced by questions of compatibility with paints, sealers, and preservatives that have been used previously, or may be used subsequently. These questions make it more difficult to define rules of thumb.

For most of us, the choice of an adhesive sealant is almost an afterthought. On the way to the cash register with our latest nautical acquisition, we stop long enough to pick up a tube of something to bed it in—something that seems to have all the right "key words" printed on the container. Beginning with the silicones, we will attempt to determine what key words to look for, and we will try to establish some ground rules for choosing a bedding or sealing compound. Armed with a working knowledge of the advantages and disadvantages of each type of polymer, it is not too difficult to narrow down the choices, and to choose the best compromise.

The Silicones

RTV (room temperature vulcanizing) silicone synthetic rubber is an elastomer derived from the silicon metal found in sand. Various curing agents give silicone its characteristic smell of vinegar or ammonia, but most marine silicone sealants are of the "acetoxy-cure" variety, which give off acetic acid as they cure. These are based on technology developed in the late 1950s by a French company, Rhone-Poulenc. Regardless of the curing system, all silicones cure by reacting with moisture in the air.

Silicone caulks are commonly found in the neighborhood hardware store (where they will normally be priced lower than in marine outlets), so the temptation exists to replace the "boat" silicones with "household" lines. For belowdecks applications, the substitution might be acceptable, but the marine distributors insist that their formulations will prove to be a better long-term value. They tell us that the household silicones contain a fungicide (anti-mildew agent) that rapidly turns yellow when exposed to ultraviolet rays. The marine silicones also contain a fungicide, but employ UV-screening agents to prevent yellowing.

Perhaps the single greatest advantage of silicone adhesive sealant and the reason for its popularity in marine applications, is its fast cure time. Most silicones will "skin" (lose tackiness) in half an hour or less, and cure completely in 24 hours. Thus, a fitting can be bedded in silicone one day, and put into service the next. Silicone sealant is virtually non-shrinking, highly resilient, and retains its elasticity throughout a wide temperature range. Silicone sealants have a long service life; twenty years is the figure most often given by manufacturers.

These desirable qualities have made the silicone compounds

the nearly unanimous choice for bedding owner-installed add-on equipment, and for bedding and sealing applications on most production boats. Unfortunately, however, the silicones have some serious drawbacks as well. The silicones have the lowest adhesion coefficient of any of the three major categories of marine synthetic caulks. This makes them suspect when applied in the form of bead of caulk in working seams, or in applications where it is necessary to fill a large void.

While of low *adhesion*, the silicones exhibit high *cohesion*. This means that once cured, they form a strong, plastic mass. The qualities of good cohesion and poor adhesion are demonstrated by the fact that silicone caulk can be pulled out of a seam in one long "rope." This quality makes silicone compounds most suitable for use as a formed-in-place "gasket" under compression. A good example of this is in the case of bedding for a stanchion base, where the compound is held in place by the compression of the mechanical fasteners.

Another notable drawback of the silicones is their absolute refusal to hold paint. Many of the silicone suppliers do not state this very clearly on their containers and some frustrating situations have been created. We have heard of numerous instances where boatowners have missed or misunderstood the warning to "paint before applying" and splashed silicones around carelessly because they planned to paint afterward. Their biggest shock came, after laboriously removing the excess, to find that an oily residue from the silicone caulk had soaked into the fiberglass, rendering it almost permanently unpaintable. There are cleaners used in the auto-painting business to remove silicone waxes prior to painting automobiles that will help (DuPont's *Prep Sol*, and Martin Senour's *Kleanz Easy*), but the silicone residue can continue to leach out of a wood or fiberglass surface for years. The use of silicone waxes and sealants is one reason why an epoxy barrier coat or an epoxy primer is almost universally recommended under polyurethane paints on fiberglass hulls and decks.

On wooden boats, where painting falls under the heading of "routine maintenance," it would be wise to avoid the use of products containing silicone altogether. If you use silicone caulk on a fiberglass boat, complete any painting that may be necessary before using silicone. Be careful about excess, and wipe it up immediately with a dry cloth or paper towel. Don't allow the excess to set, with the intention of trimming it off later. This allows more time for the silicone to invade the fiberglass, jeopardizing future paint adherence.

Paint is not the only material that does not adhere well to silicone; *silicone* does not adhere well to silicone. A damaged seam sealed with polysulfide or polyurethane, for example, can be repaired with the same material once the damaged material has been sanded or cut away. On the contrary, when replacing a fitting bedded in silicone, all of the old material should be removed, the mating surfaces cleaned, and the part should be completely rebedded in fresh material. A "smear-around-the-edges" solution to a leak is an unseamanlike procedure at best. With silicone sealants, it is likely to be a short-lived solution.

It is easy to be confused by the fact that most manufacturers' literature will advise against the use of silicone sealants below the waterline in one paragraph, and recommend silicone for bedding plastic through-hull fittings in another. The prohibition against the use of silicone underwater is designed to discourage its use as a seam-sealer due to its poor adhesion (which gets noticeably poorer after prolonged continuous exposure to water). To avoid problems, most manufacturers would prefer that customers purchase their polyurethane and polysulfide sealants for use underwater, but these compounds are not compatible with all plastics. Since poor adhesion is not a problem when silicone is used in compression under a mechanically fastened through-hull fitting, silicone becomes the recommended sealant for these fittings by default.

Before it begins to set up, silicone sealants can be tooled effectively by smoothing with a finger and wiped up with a dry cloth. Paint thinner or mineral spirits is helpful for clean-up once the material begins to cure. Once fully cured, soaking in mineral spirits will help to soften the compound for mechanical removal by cutting, scraping, and rubbing with a course cloth.

Silicones come in "clear" and a variety of colors. They are recommended for formed-in-place engine gaskets that must withstand high temperatures; for bedding deck fittings that may have to be removed at a later date; for bedding securely fastened underwater fittings of polycarbonate plastics (ABS, Lexan, PVC, acrylic) that would react unfavorably with other adhesive sealants; for potting electrical junctions (for insulation and corrosion prevention); and for sealing narrow, mechanically fastened joints in cabin joinery.

Silicones are not sandable, and should not be used where painting is required. They are susceptible to a naturally occurring bacteria (*bacillus niger*) which can cause discoloration and deterioration. They are not highly resistant to solvent contact on prolonged exposure, and are not recommended for filling large voids, or for working seams.

The Polysulfides

Polysulfide bedding and bonding materials have been in use since World War II when they were developed by Morton Thiokol for the manufacture of "leak-proof, explosion-proof" aircraft fuel tanks. During the war, aircraft crews learned that "Thiokol" was ideal for quickly patching bullet holes in planes before sending them back into the air. Polysulfide adhesive sealant is still often referred to as "Thiokol," and the polysulfide polymer in all brands of polysulfide adhesive sealant is still manufactured by Morton Thiokol, Inc.

The first widespread use of polysulfides in boatbuilding was as a bonding and sealing agent between the planks in lapstrake wooden boats in the late 1950s. Remarkably, one large manufacturer, in order to test the effectiveness of the Thiokols, built a 26-foot lapstrake boat, removed all the mechanical fasteners in the hull, and ran the boat through an entire season of hard use with no separation or leaks developing.

Many experts feel that due to its combination of high bond-strength and high elasticity, polysulfide is superior to epoxy for the bedding of teak-strip decks laid over steel, plywood, or fiberglass, regardless of whether or not mechanical fasteners are used. In any event, polysulfide is the nearly unanimous choice for the seams in both laid and overlaid decks, due to its resistance to fuels and solvents in general, and to teak cleaners in particular.

Polysulfide adhesive sealants are available in both one- and two-part formulations, but boatowners seldom run across the two-part type; it is more commonly marketed to boatbuilders and boatyards. Polysulfide is available in various consistencies; from "pourable" (the thickness of honey), to "gun-grade" (applied through a caulking cartridge); to a thick, "knife-grade" (applied with a putty knife). While somewhat less elastic than the silicones, the polysulfides retain their flexibility throughout their useful life of up to about twenty years. This quality makes these materials ideal for working seams. Their strong adhesion, plus elasticity, makes for truly permanent joints.

The polysulfides cure slowly compared with other marine adhesive sealants, with the one-part formulations generally taking significantly longer than the two-part compounds. Thiokol-based sealants cure by exposure to moisture, and thus set more quickly in high relative humidity. The curing time is also affected by ambient temperature (the warmer the temperature, the faster the cure). Although the compound should be applied to a dry surface, polysulfides will continue to cure underwater, and boats can be launched with mechanically fastened fittings bedded in partially cured material. In an emergency, polysulfides can even be applied underwater, but this should be considered a temporary fix rather than a permanent solution.

Tack-free times for one-part polysulfide reported by the manufacturers vary from as low as 30 minutes to as high as 48-72 hours; reported cure times vary upwards from 2-3 days to 7-10 days. Of course, "tack-free" involves a somewhat subjective judgement; and since the material is inherently flexible, it is often difficult to feel the material and decide whether it is "fully cured" or just "nearly cured."

Unlike the silicones, the polysulfides are sandable, although to avoid breaking the bond with the substrate, it is important that the material be fully cured before sanding. In cases where sanding is anticipated, it may be helpful to prepare a test panel at the time of caulking to use in determining if the material is fully cured and ready for sanding. In most bedding applications, however, no sanding will be required, as the uncured material can be effectively "tooled" with a rag or putty knife wet with mineral spirits. Most manufacturers recommend that wooden parts be masked with tape if the excess material is to be tooled rather than sanded. This helps to prevent the compound from becoming lodged in the surface grain of the wood.

Also in contrast to silicone sealants, polysulfides are readily paintable with no special priming required. Manufacturers' instruction differ, however, on whether the material can be painted at the "tack-free" stage, or if it should be fully cured before painting. The "primers" for polysulfide that are occasionally seen on the shelves of chandleries, incidentally, are not for the priming of polysulfide sealants prior to painting; they are for priming the surface of oily woods prior to applying the polysulfide. Trim made of teak (the archetypal "oily wood") need not be primed when it is bedded in polysulfide and mechanically fastened to a hull or deck. (In this case, the sealant is functioning simply as a gasket.) When applied as *bead* of caulk in a hull or deck *seam*, however, the adhesion of any sealant is critical, and priming is an important step. It should be noted that seams may be "oily" and thus require priming because of the nature of the material, as in the case of teak. Or the wood may be oily because of its exposure to other materials, as in the case of seams in the bilge of a wooden boat which have soaked up oily bilge water or previously used oil-based seam compounds.

The clean-up of uncured polysulfide can be accomplished easily with mineral spirits or naptha (lighter fluid). Once the material begins to set up, stronger commercial solvents such as xylol, toluene, or methyl ethyl ketone may be required. Once polysulfide is fully cured, mechanical removal is usually necessary, by cutting, scraping or sanding.

Polysulfides will adhere to metal, glass, fiberglass, wood, or any combination of these. They should not be used for cementing PVC, acrylic (Plexiglas), ABS, or Lexan plastics, because the solvents in polysulfides can leach the plasticizer from these plastics and cause them to harden and crack. Silicone sealants are usually recommended by the manufacturers of products made from these plastics. The higher-quality plastic fittings made from Delrin, nylon, glass-reinforced nylon (Marelon), or glass-filled epoxy are not affected by polysulfide sealants.

The polysulfides are not resistant to high temperatures, but are all but impervious to fuel and solvent deterioration. This makes them suitable for formed-in-place gaskets for refrigeration equipment, fuel tanks, and fuel systems. Polysulfides are particularly suitable for bedding teak, and for bedding fittings around areas of possible fuel spills. They are an excellent bedding material for underwater fittings, with the exception of the plastics noted previously. Although their adhesion is not as great as that of the polyurethanes, this is a plus, when used on fittings that might have to be removed at some time in the future.

The Polyurethanes

The polyurethanes are adhesive sealants with the accent on the word *adhesive*. Although they are highly effective as waterproof and weatherproof sealants, polymer chemists routinely refer to urethanes as "adhesives" rather than sealants or bedding compounds—in much the same way that they refer to the epoxies. In fact, the definition, "tough, flexible, waterproof, gap-filling, permanent adhesive," could apply equally well to either epoxy or polyurethane.

The owner of a fiberglass boat who does his own maintenance will find few, if any, applications for polyurethane compounds that cannot be handled effectively with polysulfides and silicones. For boat building and extensive modification projects, however, polyurethanes are "state-of-the-art" for applications that call for a permanent, self-adhesive, waterproof gasket. The common examples are the installation of chainplates, ballast keels, centerboard trunks, and hull-to-deck joints.

This is not to suggest that polyurethanes are for use by professionals only, and should not be used by the boatowner. But the boatowner who chooses to use the material should do so with the knowledge that parts bedded in polyurethane are not just *difficult* to remove, they can be nearly *impossible* to remove without damage to the part, the substrate, or both.

The polyurethanes, like the polysulfides, are available in both one- and two-part formulations, but the one-part formulation is far more commonly available in boatyards and marine outlets. Also like polysulfides, most urethanes are moisture-cured, but at least one (PRC's PR-5365-M) cures by reacting with oxygen in the air. Cure times for polyurethanes are generally longer than the silicones and shorter than the polysulfides. Polyurethanes will cure in a broad range of temperatures, but like the polysulfides, the actual cure time is a function of temperature, humidity, and the volume or surface area of the adhesive. Tack-free times at 75 degrees F and 50-percent relative humidity given by the manufacturers range from 30 minutes for Sika's Sikaflex 241, to as much as 48 hours for 3M Company's Marine 5200 Adhesive/Sealant. Three days is given as the cure time for most urethanes, with 5200 the slowest at 7 days.

Another notable similarity between the polysulfides and the polyurethanes is that they can both be sanded and painted. Some manufacturers recommend wet sanding of cured urethane, which serves as a tip-off that the urethanes do not sand easily. The flexibility of the two materials is also similar, but cured polyurethane is generally not as resilient as polysulfide. Polysulfides exhibit a fairly consistent degree of "rubberiness," and are markedly less flexible than the silicones. The flexibility of the polyurethanes, while similar to that of the polysulfides, seems to vary more from one brand to another. They range from "about as flexible" to "decidedly less flexible" than the polysulfides.

The prohibition against the use of polyurethanes for bedding thermoplastic fittings is the same as for polysulfides, but interestingly, the problem is exactly the opposite. Solvents, leaching from some plastics, can react with polyurethanes and cause a failure of the adhesive sealant compound. The end result, of course, is the same: a failed bond and hard-to-pin-down leaks.

A final area of similarity between the polysulfides and the polyurethanes is in the tooling and clean-up procedures. Before polyurethane begins to skin over, it can be tooled and removed with a rag wet with mineral spirits. The mineral spirits does not seem to dissolve the compound, but it does seem to lubricate the surface of the tool, or the area surrounding a bedded fitting enough so that the rag can "push" the excess away. Once the material begins to set up, the same industrial solvents recommended for polysulfide (xylol; toluene; methyl ethyl ketone; 1,1,1-trichloroethane) are required to remove it; once fully cured, these solvents will be of some help in softening the compound for mechanical removal.

A major difference between polyurethane and polysulfide centers around their use as a seam-sealer in teak decks. While polysulfides are specifically recommended *for* this application, most manufacturers issue warnings *against* the use of polyurethane for teak decks. 3M's 5200, for instance, carries this typical

Figure 1-2. Recommended Uses for
Synthetic Rubber-Based Adhesive Sealants

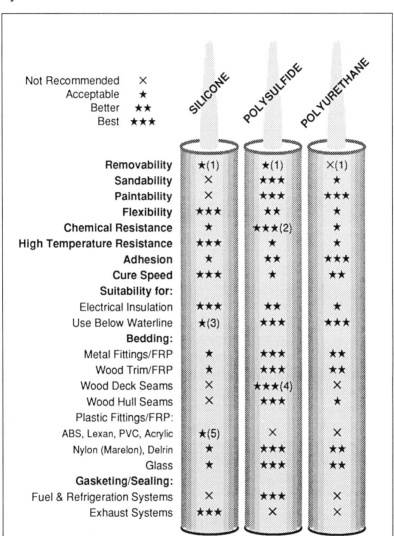

	SILICONE	POLYSULFIDE	POLYURETHANE
Not Recommended ✕			
Acceptable ★			
Better ★★			
Best ★★★			
Removability	★(1)	★(1)	✕(1)
Sandability	✕	★★★	★
Paintability	✕	★★★	★★★
Flexibility	★★★	★★	★
Chemical Resistance	★	★★★(2)	★
High Temperature Resistance	★★★	★	★
Adhesion	★	★★	★★★
Cure Speed	★★★	★	★★
Suitability for:			
Electrical Insulation	★★★	★★	★
Use Below Waterline	★(3)	★★★	★★★
Bedding:			
Metal Fittings/FRP	★	★★★	★★
Wood Trim/FRP	★	★★★	★★
Wood Deck Seams	✕	★★★(4)	✕
Wood Hull Seams	✕	★★★	★
Plastic Fittings/FRP:			
ABS, Lexan, PVC, Acrylic	★(5)	✕	✕
Nylon (Marelon), Delrin	★	★★★	★★
Glass	★	★★★	★★
Gasketing/Sealing:			
Fuel & Refrigeration Systems	✕	★★★	✕
Exhaust Systems	★★★	✕	✕

(1) Silicone and polysulfides are removable with some difficulty, polyurethane is
virtually non-removable.
(2) Polysulfides are preferred in area subject to fuel spills, teak cleaners, etc.
(3) Use silicone only for well secured plastic parts, not for working seams.
(4) Polysulfide preferred for bedding teak as 2-part teak cleaners will permanently
soften polyurethane.
(5) Silicone preferred subject to limitations discussed in text.

warning: "Not recommended for sealing wood deck seams because it may be permanently softened by certain teak cleaners." A notable exception to this prohibition is Sikaflex 231 which, according to a Sika Corporation brochure, is: "...formulated for use as a wood-deck-seam sealant for teak and mahogany decks." The same brochure, however, goes on to say, "Test Sikaflex 231 for compatibility with wood cleaners, conditioners, and paints." Given the problems of having to purchase, and then test a variety of teak cleaners, this warning would encourage us to "stick" with polysulfide for bedding and sealing teak.

An occasional splash of fuel should not affect cured polyurethane, but repeated or continuous exposure will soften the material. This is another reason why polyurethane is not recommended for bedding deck seams, and why polysulfides are preferred for seals and gaskets in fuel systems.

Polyurethane is not the "ideal" bedding and seam-sealing compound. While polyurethane adhesive sealants are not "glass-like" in rigidity, a little more flexibility would be desirable for use in working seams, although their superior adhesion makes this problem more of a theoretical than a practical one. Polyurethane adhesive sealants are definitely not for bedding parts that need routine replacement, for emergency repairs, or for rush jobs. Polyurethane is, however, the material of choice for installations that are considered permanent, or where the construction prevents proper mechanical fastening. They can be sanded and painted, used above or below the waterline, and will adhere tenaciously to glass, wood, metal, and fiberglass. The boatowner will have to judge for himself when, and if, the superadhesive power of polyurethane is required.

Recommendations/Summary

So which tube do you pick up next time on your way to the cash register? The simplest answer is: For bedding, choose between polysulfide and silicone; for seam-sealing, choose between polysulfide and polyurethane.

The polysulfides probably come closest to meeting all of the requirements of a marine adhesive sealant, and due to their superior chemical-resistance are the "safe" alternative in most cases with the exception of polycarbonate plastics. One-part polysulfide would be our first choice for the bedding of exterior teak trim, and two-part polysulfide is our choice for seam-sealing in wood hulls and decks. Slow curing is the primary drawback of the polysulfides.

The silicones are the first choice where heat-resistance is a factor, and for the bedding of mechanically fastened polycarbonate plastics. Silicone is acceptable for use underwater when the sealant is under compression, but due to its low adhesion, should not be used as a caulking compound for underwater seams. Silicone should not be used when sanding or painting will be required.

The polyurethanes are preferred where adhesion is of primary importance, and where the joint will be considered permanent. As such, we feel that polyurethanes are primarily a boat *construction* material rather than a *maintenance* material. Although some manufacturers give a qualified recommendation to their polyurethanes for seam-sealing in wooden hulls and decks, others cite greater chemical-resistance as their reason for recommending the polysulfides. In general, because items of deck hardware are routinely replaced during the life of a boat, the greatest advantage of the polyurethanes—the fact that they form a permanent bond—is also their greatest disadvantage for use as a bedding compound.

Although it is clear that no "universal" compound exists; it is equally clear that between the silicones, the polysulfides, and the polyurethanes, a long-term solution is available for all bedding and seam-sealing problems.

2

Tools and Techniques

OUTSTANDING TOOLS
FOR THE HANDY BOATOWNER

In ten years of rather serious messing about in boats, the *Practical Sailor* shop has become home to an extensive array of tools. These tools range in size and sophistication from a 500-pound Delta Unisaw to a half-dozen cast-off dental probes.

Some of these tools have earned their keep many times over. Others, we admit, have been a waste of money. Here are a few items we place high on our list of Outstanding Tools for the Handy Boatowner.

Fuller Counterbores, Tapered Drills, and Plug Cutters

The W. L. Fuller Company is a small, family-operated manufacturer of specialized cutting tools. Best known among these are their tapered drills and combination countersink/counterbores, which come in sizes for screws from #5 to #18. In a single operation, they drill a tapered pilot hole for a wood screw, as well as cut a countersink for a flush fastener, or a counterbore for a recessed and plugged screw head. The length of the drill assembly adjusts in seconds for fasteners of different lengths.

The companion to these counterbores is the Fuller plug cutter, a four-flute cutter that can easily be resharpened on a grinding wheel.

Fuller Tool earned a special position in the boatowner's pantheon by making up a custom, 5-foot by 7/8-inch drill bit for us when we had to drill out a corroded keelbolt. The 4-foot shank of the bit was turned undersized by a few thousandths on a lathe to reduce friction, and the end of the shank was turned down to

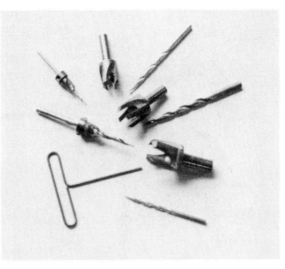

Fuller counterbores, tapered drills, and plug cutters.

fit a heavy-duty 1/2-inch drill chuck. They lost money on the deal, but it worked like a charm.

In addition to the standard countersinks designed for wood screws, Fuller makes a variety of specialized cutters, such as metal cutting countersinks and counterbores for cutting flat-bottomed recesses.

Makita Cordless Drill
Cordless drills with rechargeable power packs have been around for a long time. Most of them, unfortunately, have very little power and will not drill many holes without recharging.

Makita, a Japanese electric tool manufacturer, invaded the U.S. less than a decade ago with an incredibly diverse line of reasonably priced electric hand tools, many of them of industrial quality. A number of tools in the line are cordless, and use interchangeable battery packs.

The small 6010DWK has been a workhorse around our shop for more than five years, and is still going strong on the original power pack. Recently, we also purchased the more powerful 6012, which is a better choice for heavy-duty work. The purchase of a cordless drill will make you wonder how you lived without one, since you can do a variety of jobs on the boat when shore power is not available.

A Bosch orbital-action saber saw.

Bosch Saber Saw

The Bosch 1581VS is a new addition to the shop, but a rather remarkable one. It has the same relationship to the $39.95 saber saw you buy at the discount store that a $5 hand-held calculator does to an IBM 370. It cuts 1/2-inch aluminum cleanly and quickly, and refuses to bog down even in heavy lumber. If you were allowed only one power tool in your shop, this would probably be the one to choose.

Does it last? We recently saw a Bosch saber saw in the boatbuilding shop of Eric Goetz. The saw was one of the first electric tools in his inventory when he started building custom IOR boats a decade ago. It has been used by dozens of workers of various degrees of skill on dozens of boats in that period, and it is still going strong.

With a list price of over $200 it had better to a great job for many years. And it does.

Right-Angle Drill Attachment

Somewhere, you have to draw the line on spending money on tools. We have certainly explored beyond that line on a number of occasions, but not on this one.

Aboard a boat, you sometimes have to drill a hole in a cramped space that does not allow you to get an ordinary electric

A cabinetmaker's screwdriver.

drill in at a decent angle. The result is often a hole drilled at an improper angle, and a fastener that does not bear the way it should. The best answer is a slim right-angle electric drill, but most boatowners would find it difficult to justify the expense of an additional drill.

The compromise is an inexpensive, right-angle attachment you can buy at any hardware store for under $10. The only drawback is that you need to scavenge a drill chuck from somewhere to put on the end of the spindle. Almost every shop has an old electric drill that has outlived its useful life. If it has a decent Jacobs chuck, however, you can easily remove it and install it on your right-angle attachment.

Because it takes two hands to use this tool properly in an ordinary drill, it is not really good for continuous duty. But for the occasional hole in a tight place, a right-angle attachment makes more sense than spending a lot of money on a specialized tool that may not get used very often.

Cabinetmaker's Screwdriver

What could be more prosaic than a screwdriver? Not much, and you probably have a drawer full of them. If all you have to do is hold the head of a machine screw, which is fairly effortless until the nut fetches up, a plastic-handled screwdriver is fine.

Cork sanding blocks cut from old cork-filled life preservers.

Wood screws are another matter. To hold their best, they must fit tightly in the pilot holes you have drilled with your Fuller tapered bits, so driving a wood screw takes a fair amount of force from start to finish. Try driving a few hundred #12 screws with an ordinary screwdriver, and you will probably have blisters the size of quarters.

A cabinetmaker's screwdriver, with its large, smooth wooden handle, will raise far fewer blisters on the palm of your hand while enabling you to keep good pressure on the fastener. The upper part of the shank is flattened so you can fit a wrench over it to apply a lot of torque when necessary, such as when backing out a seized fastener.

Cork Sanding Blocks

Now we are really getting basic. Commercial sanding blocks are usually designed to use long, narrow strips of sandpaper. You waste a fair amount of the sheet at each end of the strip, where it fits into the slots that hold the sandpaper on the block.

You can make a great sanding block from a thick piece of cork cut from an old cork life preserver. The cork is rigid, and therefore is good for fairing flat surfaces, which develop hollows and high spots if sanded without a block.

Cut the block so that a half sheet of sandpaper fits it exactly. This way, you get two wide surfaces for each half sheet of paper, plus two narrow ones on the edges of the block. When the paper on the two larger surfaces is used up, you can shift the position of the paper on the block to bring a smaller fresh surface to bear—with absolutely no wasted paper.

Put your name on them with a felt-tipped marker because other boatowners will try to borrow them. And here's a bonus: If you drop your cork sanding block over the side, it will float; your rubber sanding block will sink like a stone.

CHOOSE THE RIGHT POWER SANDER FOR THE JOB

One of the grand illusions of the fiberglass revolution was the welcome relief from tedious maintenance chores associated with owning a wooden boat. Alas, it was illusion. Two decades later, we are still sanding, varnishing, painting, overhauling engines, and doing the dozens of other chores that make owning a boat a delight to some, a burden to others.

The first fiberglass boats had very little wood, and true to the promise, not much painting or varnishing was required on those austere craft; they deserved the term "Clorox bottle," which they inspired. Most of us, however, found little to admire about a boat with no wood. As a result, boats acquired more and more exterior wood trim over the years—wood toe rails, wood hatches, and even wood decks. Now many fiberglass boats have as much exterior wood on them as the typical wooden boat of thirty years ago.

Where there is wood, there is maintenance. Where there is maintenance, there is the need to sand things. When you need to sand things, you look for shortcuts to relieve the tedium. With sanding, the shortcut is the power sander.

There are literally hundreds of power sanding tools on the market, ranging in price from under $25 to well over $200. Some will make maintaining a boat easier. Some have the potential to do hundreds of dollars of damage to your boat in a few moments of inattention. None is idiot-proof. The choice of the right sander for the job can make all the difference, not only in the time it takes to get the job done, but in the quality of the finished project. Before looking at the costs and characteristics of individual types of sanders, let's discuss the basics.

If you have wooden hatches on your boat, there is a good chance that they are veneered plywood, rather than solid lumber. Likewise, the teak companionway dropboards on your boat are about as likely to be teak veneer plywood as they are to be solid teak. The cost of your boat does not determine whether they are solid lumber or veneer; Nautor sometimes uses plywood dropboards on its Swan line of boats, and so does Tartan.

Veneered surfaces that are to be finished bright (varnished or oiled) are usually not suited to power sanding. The veneer is simply too thin for more than the lightest hand-sanding. A simple rule of thumb is that if you have teak veneered surfaces on the outside of the boat, they should be varnished rather than oiled, unless you want to replace them every few years.

The risk of damage to your boat from the improper use of a sander is directly proportional to the speed at which the sander operates. While this may seem self-evident, think about it the next time you are looking for a faster way to remove bottom paint or sand down your badly worn toe rails. We have all heard stories of boats with bottoms ruined by an inexperienced operator with a flexible disk sander. With these caveats in mind, here are a variety of sanders for use on your boat, and a brief description of the proper use of each type.

Belt Sander

In the hands of an experienced operator, the belt sander is one of the fastest, most useful of power tools. In the hands of the inexperienced, it is one of the fastest ways to ruin the value of your boat short of running it onto a reef.

Belt sanders are useful only for relatively large, flat surfaces. On most boats, this means teak decks, hatch tops (provided they are solid lumber) wide rail caps, and box-section wooden spars. While a belt sander can be used to remove paint or varnish, it is best to strip the surfaces to be sanded before using a belt sander.

An inexpensive belt sander is ideal for sanding large, flat areas.

It is very easy to dig a hole in a surface with a belt sander while trying to remove the last bit of varnish from a spruce mast or a teak hatch cover.

Except for truing up new surfaces, such as newly-laid teak decks or new hatch covers, you will rarely need to use a sanding belt coarser than 120 grit. Because a belt sander removes so much material so quickly, think of the coarseness of the paper used as being twice that of the same grit paper used by hand or in an orbital sander. If you would use 60-grit paper in an orbital sander to do the job you are contemplating, then use a 120-grit belt in the belt sander.

Despite the fact that a belt sander has a large, flat sanding area, it is extremely difficult to keep the sander flat on a surface that has large irregularities. A newly glued-up hatch top may have great globs of glue squeezed out of the joints, for example, and a teak deck is likely to have ridges of seam compound. Unless you are very handy with a belt sander, remove these major surface irregularities first, using a chisel, a scraper, or by hand sanding. This will help to prevent grooves in the surface from the edge of the sanding belt as the sander tips from side to side. Removing these grooves may require taking a lot of wood off the surface.

The belt sander should always be used parallel to the grain of the wood, to avoid cross-grain scratches which are difficult to sand out. Never try to sand too close to a piece of hardware that cannot be removed for sanding. You will almost inevitably end up with a hollow at the end of your sanding stroke. Above all, practice on a scrap surface before attacking your boat. It is far cheaper to ruin a few pieces of pine than it is to ruin a hatch cover.

Forget about $29.95 belt sanders. We would not recommend a belt sander of less than one horsepower or one that uses a belt smaller than 3 by 21 inches. A good one will retail for $100 to $200, and will pay for itself in a day if you have a lot of large, flat surfaces to sand.

Disk Sanders

While most people have a healthy fear of belt sanders and the damage they can do, they may not appreciate the potential of the disk sander as a tool of destruction. Perhaps this is because almost all of us, at one time or another, have used a hard-rubber sanding disk in the chuck of an electric drill, probably without disastrous results. Using a large, foam-backed pad in a heavy-duty disk sander would seem to be simple by comparison. Unfortunately, this is not necessarily so.

The disk sander we are referring to here is an industrial-grade tool referred to as a sander/polisher or a disk grinder. Those models referred to as sander/polishers run at relatively slow speeds—less than 3,500 rpm—while grinders run at speeds of up to 10,000 rpm. The high-speed grinder is a cutting tool for removing metal or fiberglass; the slower speed models are preferable for most jobs you are likely to do aboard a boat.

The most common use on a boat for the disk sander is to remove bottom paint, but its usefulness for this task varies with the type of bottom paint, the tool used, and the skill of the operator. In our experience, vinyl and chlorinated rubber bottom paints sand very poorly with a disk sander. These paints tend to melt or polish, rather than to sand off, clogging sanding disks in short order. Attempting to sand these paints results in a surface that may have poorer adhesion for future coats of paint than a surface that is merely scrubbed with a stiff brush and washed off.

For removing bottom paint, the disk sander should be equipped with an 8-inch medium-density foam pad. The entire sanding pad must be kept flat on the surface being sanded to avoid leaving gouges. Unfortunately, the disk sander is easier to control if it is tilted slightly, but you will ruin the bottom of your boat if you use it this way. You can either cut your own disks for this pad from standard 9- by 11-inch sheets of sandpaper, or you can buy precut, self-adhesive sanding disks. Unless you really know what you are doing, don't use an electric disk sander for sanding the topsides.

Experienced professionals sometimes use a disk sander equipped with a large-diameter hard rubber pad. On a wooden hull, this is an excellent tool both for removing paint and for fairing an irregular surface, on either the topsides or the bottom. We can only recommend this technique for those who are highly skilled in the use of the tool.

A good disk sander will cost between $100 and $200. An 8-inch foam sanding pad costs about $20.

Finishing Sanders

The term "finishing sander" is applied to a wide variety of sanders, but we define it as a sander with a rectangular sanding surface about 4 inches by 8 inches, sanding at relatively high speed with orbital or reciprocal action. Finishing sanders are designed to be held with both hands. The finishing sander is the type that most commonly comes to mind when you think of electric sanders. You can buy a finishing sander for $19.95. You can also buy one for $150. There is probably as much difference in quality as the price difference implies.

Because the sanding pad of an orbital finishing sander travels in an orbital path, the sanded surface has minute circular scratches in it. These are most pronounced if the sander is placed on the surface and then turned on, or if it is switched off before being lifted from the surface.

Even using the sander carefully, these telltale scratches make the orbital sander inappropriate for use on a surface to be varnished. The scratches are also likely to show through a surface painted with polyurethane, since the paint is so thin that it has almost no hiding qualities.

For such jobs, the reciprocal sander can be used. The pad of a reciprocal sander travels back and forth in a straight line, and therefore it can be used on bare wood, (with the grain, naturally)

Orbital-type finishing sanders leave tiny swirl marks which invariably show through varnish or polyurethane paint.

to produce a smooth finish. Reciprocal sanders are not as commonly available as orbital sanders, however. A more specialized tool, the reciprocal sander is the slowest and least aggressive of the power sanders.

Finishing sanders are a reasonably good way to sand soft bottom paint, since the scratches in the surface are less important than in the topsides or brightwork. They can also be used with success for sanding vinyl bottom paints, since they are less prone to melt the paint than disk sanders.

As a rule, finishing sanders are much slower in removing paint than disk sanders or belt sanders. While this may make the job take longer, it also means that you are less likely to ruin your hull using a finishing sander.

Because of its relatively large sanding surface, an orbital sander can be used for slight fairing of untrue wooden surfaces, such as an irregular hatch top or toerail. If this type of surface is to be finished bright, however, it will be necessary to remove the surface scratches by sanding extensively with a reciprocal sander or by hand-sanding with a block. On a oiled surface such as a teak toerail, you may be able to get away with using an orbital sander with successively finer grits of paper to remove the most offensive scratches.

There are literally dozens of finishing sanders on the market. They are periodically tested by organizations such as Consumers' Union, which publishes *Consumer Reports*. Unfortunately, only relatively inexpensive homeowner-type sanders are usually tested, and these are usually poorly designed for hours of sanding on the bottom of a boat. Our shop contains a half dozen or more finishing sanders, but they have fallen into total disuse as our skill with more specialized tools has grown. We suspect that the same will eventually happen to your finishing sanders.

Palm Sanders

Palm sanders are smaller, lighter-weight orbital sanders. They are frequently called finishing sanders, too. The type name derives from the fact that they are designed to be held in the palm of one hand, rather than both hands. Typically, a palm sander uses a quarter sheet of sandpaper, and sands with an orbital action. Most have a list price of $80 to $100 and are available from mail-order tool outlets for about $50 or $60.

The original palm sander is the Rockwell or Porter-Cable Speedblock. In our experience, this is a heavy tool, and transmits a lot of vibration to the hand of the operator. However, it sands well, with the same limitations on sanding surfaces to be varnished as other types of orbital sanders.

The new generation of palm sanders is represented by the Makita BO4510. This extremely compact and lightweight palm sander is in our experience both more reliable, easier to use, and a better sanding machine than the old generation of palm sanders. Despite the light weight and not particularly robust-looking construction, the two Makitas we have used for the last five years have never faltered, despite ridiculous demands made on them.

The acceptance of the compact Makita sander has spawned a number of similar tools from other manufacturers, including Ryobi, Hitachi, Black & Decker, and Sears. Although we have tried some of these, none seems any better than the Makita.

The palm sander is used in much the same way as any other finishing sander. However, being lighter, it is easier to use for long periods of time, particularly when sanding overhead. In addition, the Makita seems to sand faster than other finishing sanders of the same price, and seems to leave fewer swirl marks in the surface. It does not eliminate swirl marks, however, and hand finishing will still be required on surfaces to be varnished or painted with polyurethane.

Another advantage of the palm sander is that it uses a quarter of a sheet of sandpaper, resulting in practically no waste at all. This is truly a versatile sanding tool.

Pneumatic Tools

Much of the professional sanding in the world is done with air-powered tools. Air-powered tools have a number of advantages. You can use them for wet sanding, since there is no electric motor to short out. The lack of an electric motor also means no failures due to a burned out motor. Many air-powered sanding tools were originally developed for the automotive industry, where a good finish is critical. Professional-grade pneumatic tools generally cut faster and cost less than their electric counterparts.

The drawback to air-powered tools is that you need a compressor in order to use them. A pneumatic sander typically requires 8 cubic feet of air per minute at a pressure of 90 pounds per square inch. This means you need at least a 2-horsepower compressor, costing several hundred dollars, to run a single sanding tool. As a result, pneumatic tools are prohibitively expensive for most boatowners.

*   *   *

If we had to get by with only one electric sander, it would be a palm sander such as the Makita BO4510. But power sanders can save so much time that the expense of several types is justified if you have a lot of wood on your boat.

We have never seen an electric sander which yields a good enough surface for varnishing without final sanding by hand. We do our hand sanding with half sheets of paper wrapped around a cork block.

On surfaces having a slight curvature, such as topsides, we use a dense-rubber sanding block, which costs about $4 at any hardware store. Another specialized sanding block for fairing large surfaces, called a "long board," can be made from very thin plywood with neoprene glued to the surface, around which sandpaper can be wrapped and stapled. Wooden handles are usually screwed to the tops of these blocks to make them easier to handle.

Except for sanding between coats of paint or varnish, hand sanding without a block is a poor idea. Even the irregularities in pressure over the surface of your hand introduces some unevenness in the surface being sanded. Compounded over the years, small irregularities can add up to big ones.

Sanding is not a glamorous job; few people will compliment you on a well-sanded toerail or hatch cover. Nevertheless, sanding is the key to the quality of the finished surface. Good sanding skills, and good sanding tools can add greatly to the pride you take in your boat.

BUILD AN INEXPENSIVE POLISHER

When you think about the characteristics of a good-looking yacht, you probably think about gleaming topsides, golden-yellow teak, and metal hardware polished to a high sheen. Highly polished hardware does not only reflect the pride of the boatowner, however; it is also safer and more functional.

Bronze, for example, is a fairly soft metal, but it is still much harder than your docklines and anchor rode. A poorly polished chock can wear through a heavy nylon line astonishingly fast in heavy weather. With stainless steel hardware, a poorly polished surface can lead to crevice corrosion, which could eventually result in the failure of a piece of hardware under stress.

Hours of hand-polishing is not always necessary to make metal objects gleam like new (or to make new items gleam like they should). An inexpensive polishing wheel on an electric motor whirring away at 2,000 RPM, can quickly cut many polishing jobs down to size.

If you already own a bench grinder, you can easily reap the benefits of the polisher at minimum cost. At any good hardware store, you can buy buffing wheels 4, 6, or 8 inches in diameter, depending on the capacity of your grinder. You simply remove one of the grinding wheels, and slip the buffing wheel on. For the confirmed tinkerer with metal, however, it may make more sense to make up a tool totally dedicated to polishing. It will be the simplest power tool in your workshop.

The basic components of an electric motor, a buffing wheel, and a work arbor (if necessary) for mounting of the wheel.

To start, you need an electric motor. Fortunately, our society runs on electric motors. They power the compressors in our refrigerators, the drums in our clothes driers; the electric motor is ubiquitous—and cheap.

An electric motor for a polisher can be as small as 1/4 horsepower, although 1/2 horsepower is about the ideal size. Since there is almost no starting load on the motor (it does not have to turn pulleys or drive belts) an inexpensive split-phase motor can be used, rather than a more expensive capacitor-start motor. The motor should have a 1/2-inch or 5/8-inch shaft, since that is the arbor size of most buffing wheels. Adaptors are available to convert a 1/2-inch shaft to the larger size. A used motor is fine, and can probably be purchased from an electric motor service company for $25, or at a flea market for less than that. If you would prefer to order a new motor, the Sears model 9-HT-1285C is a reasonable choice.

If your motor has a mounting base (a metal frame attached to the motor with holes to allow it to be bolted down), you are

A pull-on, push-off switch designed for stationary power tools is a valuable safety feature of the polisher.

almost in business. If it does not, you can make one in a few minutes. Cut a cradle from two pieces of scrap wood about 3/4 inch thick. A semicircular cutout, the diameter of the motor casing, is made in each piece of wood. These two end pieces are, in turn, attached to a base of plywood about ten inches square. The motor is held in the cradle using plumber's perforated pipe-strap, which can be cut to any length to suit.

It may be necessary to install a shaft collar on the motor shaft, unless there is already one there. This is simply a metal collar that slips over the shaft and is held in place by a set screw. It serves as an inside stop for the metal arbor of the polishing wheel, to hold it in position on the shaft. If there are no threads cut in the end of the shaft for a retaining nut, another collar can be fitted on the other side of the wheel to hold it in place. Rubber washers on the shaft on either side of the wheel should provide enough friction to hold the wheel in place. Or, if there is a keyway milled in the motor shaft, you can cut a keyway in the buffing wheel arbor to match, and insert a piece of key stock of the proper size.

For a temporary installation, the base of the polisher can be clamped to a sturdy table or workbench, making sure that the clamps are positioned so they are not in the way of the buffing operations. For a permanent installation, bolt the base to the end of a workbench. The buffing wheel should project past the end of the bench to allow you to get fairly large pieces up to the wheel.

Ideally, you should install a switch in the power line. A pull on/push off switch, designed specifically for use with stationary power tools, is the best way to go. Sears model 9-HT-13632 switch is a good choice. In an emergency, a push off switch is the easiest kind to trip.

The height of the motor relative to the base or workbench controls how large a buffing wheel you can use. As a rule, use the biggest wheel you can. This may mean blocking up the metal mounting base of the motor before attaching it to the plywood base, or simply making the wooden cradles higher, relative to the wooden base.

Usually, you can buy polishing compounds wherever you purchase the buffing wheel. These come in different grades of abrasiveness, from emery (coarse) to rouge (fine). The finer the grit, the higher the polish. You can use successive grits of polishing compound on the same buffing wheel, but you may want to buy a second wheel which is reserved for the finest compounds. Fine polishes are especially suited to putting a gleaming finish on stainless steel fittings. A high polish on stainless can help to retard unsightly surface bleeding.

Using the polisher is simplicity itself. The polishing compound is applied to the wheel by holding a bar of polish lightly to the spinning wheel. A large workpiece can be held in the hand as you polish it. Tiny ones should be gripped with pliers. Just press the workpiece against the spinning buffing wheel, holding on tightly.

Always wear safety glasses and gloves when working with a polisher. If you are careless, the wheel can grab the workpiece and tear it from your hands. As with all power tools, there is a real risk of injury unless you give constant attention to the job!

The longer you use your polisher, the more uses you will find for it. A useful service of your polishing wheel is to remove minute steel particles from the surface of brass, bronze, and stainless. Any time you cut these metals with a hacksaw or a file (such as cutting a bolt to length), small particles of the steel tool are left on the surface. These provide most of the brown surface stains on these metals once they are exposed to salt air or water, since tool steel rusts almost instantly.

*   *   *

There is something fascinating about putting a polish on tarnished pieces of metal, something on the same level as staring into a campfire. But it is a healthy fascination, and one you can afford to indulge with no guilt at all. While you might build a polisher to use for boat hardware, you will probably find yourself buffing away on household things, too, like your copper cookware or stainless steel utensils.

3

Interior Projects and Improvements

INSTALLING A PROPANE STOVE

We often do odd things for the sake of safety. Take, for example, the time-honored American tradition of cooking with alcohol aboard boats. Conventional wisdom has it that alcohol is the only truly safe cooking fuel afloat; cook with gas and you stand a chance of blowing yourself up.

Somehow, the rest of the world has failed to get the message. Go to Europe to buy a boat, and what do you get for cooking fuel? Propane, or some other compressed gas. Go to the isolated islands of the Pacific, or the Caribbean, and what do people cook with? Propane. Charter a bareboat in St. Thomas, and what do you get to cook with? Propane.

Are you starting to get the picture? The myth that alcohol is safe and gas is dangerous has brought a higher standard of living to boatowners in the rest of the world, while American boatowners struggle along in the dark ages, nursing fragile alcohol flames for hours on end to boil a pot of water for a cup of coffee. We wait for hours for a dish of lasagna to bake while our dinner guests perish from boredom or drink themselves comatose waiting for supper to be served.

Yes, you can escape slavery to alcohol—and we don't mean the consumable type. The answer is to install a gas stove aboard your boat.

Choosing a Stove

The brand and model stove you select will depend on the size of your boat, the galley layout, the way the boat is used, and the amount of cooking you do. You can spend anything from $40 to well over $1000 for a stove, so a certain amount of planning and common sense is required.

If you have a trailer sailer that is used for weekend jaunts on a nearby lake, your cooking requirements are substantially different from someone taking off on a three-year cruise on a 40-footer. As a rule, a gimballed, multiburner stove with oven is out of place on a boat much smaller than 30 feet, unless it is used for extended cruising.

Rather than use an expensive marine stove, a small cruiser may be better off with a simple two-burner camping stove, which can easily be modified to bolt to a galley counter when in use. A basic Coleman camping stove can do all the cooking required for weekending on a small boat, and the cost is almost negligible. Unfortunately, your insurance company probably will not go for the idea of a propane camping stove used aboard a boat, for the simple reason that the standard 14-ounce fuel bottles will be used below decks. In our opinion, such a stove poses very little risk. When not in use, the self-sealing bottles can be removed from the stove and stowed on deck.

To make a camping stove even more suitable for a boat, DeGill Corporation (61 Main Street; Claremont, NH 03743) makes a set of pot holders and rails that attach to a camping stove, allowing pots to be held safely in place. At about $30, they will keep your total investment to about $70—still far less than the simplest two-burner marine alcohol stove, and light years ahead in cooking efficiency. Of course, camping stoves are made of enameled steel, and may rust out after a few years of use. At this price, however, you can afford to replace them periodically.

If your boat is already equipped with the ubiquitous recessed Kenyon two-burner alcohol stove, the company now makes an identical stove for use with propane. You cannot connect disposable propane cylinders to this stove without a pressure-reducing regulator, as the Kenyon stove is designed to work at a lower gas pressure, like other marine propane stoves. Replacing a recessed alcohol stove with a similar recessed propane stove makes for an easy installation, but the problems of fuel tank installation will be the same as for a larger stove.

It is hard to justify the complication of an external propane-tank locker on a boat small enough to have its cooking needs met by an ungimballed two-burner range top. In many cases, the actual stove installation is less than half the hassle of the total conversion to propane.

Propane really comes into its own on boats used for living aboard or for extended cruising. At the risk of sounding hope-lessly chauvinistic, it can also make the difference between a mate who enjoys cruising, and one who at best tolerates the experience. For people who spend most of their lives ashore, living aboard a boat for much more than a weekend is an expe-rience about as foreign as a trip to the moon. Think about it for a minute. There you are in a space about the size of a walk-in closet, where two, four, or even six people—perhaps including small, restless children—will eat, sleep and do everything else for an extended period of time. Every now and then, your closet tilts at about 30 degrees to the side and jumps up and down, and sometimes large quantities of water are thrown in your face, just to make life aboard more interesting. Your clothes are always damp, your bed is damp, you never have enough drawer space, closet space, counter space, or room to dress. Food rots in the re-frigerator. You have to pump water by hand to brush your teeth. You have to pump the toilet by hand. And you want someone to cook on an alcohol stove, to boot?

On a larger boat, a gas stove can make the difference between a pleasurable cruise for all aboard, and an activity which is precariously close to that bizarre form of self-punishment known as "camping out."

A stove used aboard a serious cruiser should have two or three burners, plus an oven large enough to hold more than a loaf of bread. It must be of corrosion-resistant construction, prefera-bly stainless steel. The pot grates should be bronze or stainless steel, as iron grates tend to rust quickly. There must be a sea-rail system which can be augmented with adjustable racks to hold pots in place in heavy weather.

On a sailing vessel or a displacement powerboat, the stove should be gimballed. However, a poorly gimballed stove is worse than a good fixed stove. A gimballed stove that is unstable when the oven door is opened can dump the contents of the entire stove in your lap. For this reason, ballast on the bottom is highly desirable. (If you are ballasting an existing stove, don't use lead ballast on the inside of the oven. You could contaminate your food.)

Gimballing is accomplished in a variety of ways. One of the best systems is that used by Shipmate, which incorporates two brass pillow blocks simply mounted to brackets installed in the stove well. The pillow blocks are held together with wing nuts, allowing the gimballing friction to be adjusted for different sea conditions—a highly desirable arrangement.

Ideally, the oven door should be equipped with a positive external latch. Doors relying solely on spring tension can be knocked open in heavy weather. An external oven thermometer is also desirable. The oven door should have a window to let you keep track of things without opening the door—a simple task that can be hazardous in rough conditions.

These features come at a substantial price. A good, gimballed range and oven with most of these features will cost between $800 and $1500; and that's before you have begun to add the cost of installation.

Installation

Before you buy a stove, you must determine where you are going to put it. An obvious consideration, perhaps, but one not as easily solved as it may first appear. If you are simply replacing a countertop or recessed stove with a gas version of the same stove, installation problems are minimal. However, if you plan on using disposable gas bottles below, you must make provision for securing them in place while the stove is in use. A simple wooden bracket, or even the mounting bracket from a small dry chemical fire extinguisher will serve to keep the bottle in place.

Remember, you may be on your own as far as your insurance company goes if you use disposable gas bottles, so check this out. These bottles have an enviable safety record in other uses, but are not accepted for marine use by any of the marine standard-making bodies, such as the American Boat and Yacht Council, Inc. (ABYC).

Larger gimballed stoves are almost always fitted in a well let into a galley counter. The wells we have seen on most production boats range from excellent to abysmal, so evaluate yours carefully to see what is involved in upgrading the galley stove.

The first and most obvious characteristic of the well is that the stove must fit into it. Stove dimensions are not standardized, and until you see the installation drawings for an individual stove, you don't know if the dimensions given include things like external gimbal blocks, burner controls, or other external protuberances. Don't buy a stove without first getting the installation drawing to see if it will fit in the well on your boat.

A well that is too wide is not usually a problem. Mounting brackets can be fabricated by any welding shop to mount to the sides of the well. These must be heavy-gauge stainless steel, not only for strength (a stove can weigh 100 pounds or more) but to be fire-resistant.

The most common problems with stove wells is the lack of adequate depth behind the stove for proper gimballing. Ideally, the stove should be free to gimbal a full 90 degrees, in either direction, without hitting anything. This means that you have to consider the position of any front guard rail across the well, in addition to the fore and aft depth. An installation that prevents the stove from swinging less than 45 degrees is really not acceptable, even though a stove will rarely be called upon to perform in this way. When calculating the amount of space needed for gimballing, don't forget that the fuel delivery hose must enter the well and attach to the stove. You certainly don't want the stove to pinch the hose between itself and the well when it swings.

The stove well should be completely lined with stainless steel sheet metal, and insulation should be installed behind the liner. This insulation should be asbestos board—the soft type, not the cement board, which might fracture when the boat pounds. If the asbestos is sealed thoroughly behind the sheet metal, with no edges exposed, the installation should not be a health hazard. Obviously, you must take precautions, such as wearing a good respirator, long sleeves, and gloves, when cutting and handling asbestos products. A lined and insulated stove well can offer a lot of protection to the boat in the event of a fire, giving you time to extinguish a small blaze before it spreads. This is important no matter what stove fuel is used.

The modification of a stove well to accommodate a specific stove can be a major project, particularly if the well is a fiberglass molding. Only if the galley is of wood construction is any significant change in size likely to be possible. You are better off spending time looking for a stove that fits.

Usually, the actual installation of a new stove in the stove well is one of the easier parts of the project. What you must remember is that a galley stove is heavy, and must be very securely mounted. Mounting brackets must be strongly bolted to the sides of the well. The stove should not be capable of being lifted off its gimbals or mounting brackets. These must be designed to hold the stove even if the boat is inverted, as a loose stove would be a dangerous projectile—not to mention the potentially disastrous results of a ruptured fuel hose if the stove comes adrift.

A final consideration when installing the stove is the point at which the fuel delivery hose will enter the well. Wherever it enters, it must not interfere with the gimballing of the stove, and the flexible hose cannot be allowed to chafe on anything. A large enough loop of hose must be left in the well for completely free gimballing without a pulling load on the hose. It would probably be best if the hose entered the well somewhere other than the bottom, to avoid the potential leaking of heavier-than-air propane through a fuel hose opening into another part of the boat.

Installing Fuel Tanks

Installing the fuel tank or tanks can be the hardest part of a propane stove installation. ABYC's *Standard A-1* covers the recommended installation of tanks, and the standard may be hard to comply with if the storage of propane tanks was not designed into your boat.

Propane tanks must be stored in a locker used solely for that purpose. The locker cannot be used for spare lines or fenders, and it must be isolated from any interior space in the boat. In other words, you can't just partition off part of the existing cockpit locker which is entered through one large lid. You could

A built-in propane locker, such as this molded cockpit locker, is the best solution to the propane storage problem.

modify an existing locker, however, so that the propane locker lid remains closed when you get into the regular cockpit locker.

Another possibility is to construct a deck-mounted box of wood or fiberglass, but on a small boat, the windage and bulk of such a box may be disproportionately great. Still another possibility is to build a box at the after or forward end of the cockpit, where it functions as a seat or a bridgedeck.

The advantage of a deck-mounted box is that no scuppers through the hull are required. A locker that is part of the cockpit must have an overboard drain. Draining into the cockpit is not acceptable, according to ABYC standards, although we think that with some types of cockpit construction the intent of the standard could be met.

Don't buy your propane bottles until you figure out where you are going to put them. The dimensions of bottles vary significantly with both the capacity and material of the bottle. Go to the local propane supplier to get bottle dimensions, then figure out what will fit aboard your boat.

You can buy either steel or aluminum bottles. Aluminum

Propane bottles can also be installed in deck-mounted boxes of wood or fiberglass. This one incorporates two dorade vents.

bottles are lighter and more corrosion-resistant. They also cost two to three times as much as steel, and are very slightly larger for the same capacity. Steel bottles are cheap, but you fight a constant battle with rust. If you buy steel bottles, paint them before they ever get to the boat, even though they are already painted, and touch up the paint whenever it needs it. Remember that the bottles are going to get rolled around every time they are filled, so it is unrealistic to expect the paint to last.

Whatever material you select, mounting the bottles in the locker deserves some thought. They should be firmly held in place, either by chocks or rubber wedges. Allowing steel bottles to rub against each other in a locker not only will wear out paint, but could generate a spark which could cause an explosion if there is a leak in the locker. Besides, the sound of the bottles clanking around inside a locker can drive you crazy.

If you have room for a locker that will hold two bottles, do it. Nothing is more frustrating than running out of fuel in the middle of a meal without having a new cylinder. If there isn't room for two large gas bottles, a pair of rather ingenious adaptors, called *Bird-in-the-Hand* and *Ace-in-the-Hole*, are available. They allow a one-pound (14-ounce) disposable propane bottle to be plugged into the regular propane delivery system in case you run out of fuel. Since a disposable cylinder provides a little over two hours of burner time, it could really save your bacon. The Bird-in-the-Hand incorporates a shut-off valve like the one on top of a regular propane cylinder, while the Ace-in-the-Hole is simply a straight adapter with no provision for manual shut-off. Both adapters are available from the manufacturer, Springer Company International (2101 West Burbank Boulevard; Burbank, CA 91506).

In addition to providing space for the gas bottles, the locker must hold the regulator, the pressure gauge (if one is fitted), and an electric shutoff solenoid (optional, but strongly recommended), so be sure to allow adequate space. Propane regulators are simple pot-metal items available at any gas supply house. At about $15, they can be considered expendable; they do not last long in the marine environment.

The drain for a propane locker must be at least 1/2 inch in diameter. A plastic through-hull fitting makes a good drain. The hose for the drain, which may be plastic, should lead downward and overboard through the topsides, positioned so that it is above the waterline but lower than the bottom of the gas locker at all angles of heel. This can be tricky, so plan carefully before cutting any holes. The drain should not exit the hull within two feet of an engine or generator exhaust, or in a location where propane fumes could be drawn into the boat through an open port or hatch.

A deck-mounted propane locker eliminates much of the hassle of bottle installation. On larger boats or boats with flush decks, a deck-mounted locker should be reasonably unobtrusive. The primary advantage of a deck locker is that the complicated drain system, with holes through the hull, is avoided. Adequate ventilation of a deck locker is provided by small scuppers in the top and bottom of the locker. The scuppers should total no less than one square inch of area for each seven pounds of propane carried in the locker.

The deck-mounted locker must be ruggedly constructed and securely fastened to the deck, since it is exposed to waves in heavy weather. For this reason, the locker should not be mounted at the forward end of a cabin trunk at deck level. This is the most vulnerable part of the boat sailing upwind in heavy air, as anyone who has ever carried green water on deck knows.

Solenoids

The electric shutoff solenoid has gone a long way toward making propane installations safer. This consists of an electrically-operated shutoff valve in line with the regulator, mounted in the gas storage locker. The valve is operated by a switch on a panel mounted below. Proper practice calls for operating this switch every time the gas appliance is used, turning it on for use and off immediately afterward. To be really safe, when you are finished cooking, the burner can be left on when the shutoff switch is thrown, and most of the gas in the delivery line will be burned. When the stove goes out, the burner is immediately shut off.

The switch panel for the shutoff solenoid may be mounted in the galley for the sake of convenience, but it should not be immediately adjacent to the stove. If there is a stove fire, you want to be able to get to the switch without frying yourself. At the same time, it should be visible and accessible, so the cook will not forget to throw the switch when the cooking is finished.

Plumbing

Leaks are the major concern in a propane system, so the fewer joints you have in the fuel delivery line, the better. Copper water tubing is probably the best to use for the long run between the fuel supply and the stove. We suggest using flare fittings on the copper tubing instead of compression fittings.

A section of flexible hose is used in the stove well to allow the stove to gimbal. You can have this hose made up by any company that handles gasses. Be sure that the person making up the hose understands the way it will be used. When installing the hose, check once again to be sure that there is nothing that can chafe on it as the stove swings.

It is critical that the fuel delivery tube be protected from damage throughout its length. It should not run through the bottom of lockers, nor should it rest against fasteners or other metal objects. The tubing should be supported at regular intervals either by non-metallic hangers, or metal hangers with plastic inserts. Where the tubing must pass through bulkheads, it should be protected with rubber gasketing.

*   *   *

With a careful installation and careful maintenance, a propane system is as safe as any other fuel you might use aboard a boat. Propane is not a fuel to be handled casually, however. It is heavier than air, and if leaks develop in the system, explosive pockets of propane gas can accumulate in bilges or lockers.

At the same time, the convenience of gas cooking is remarkable. Unlike alcohol or kerosene, gas fuels ignite readily with mechanical "sparkers;" no more struggling to light a soggy match in the damp, breezy marine environment. Because a gas flame burns much hotter, cooking time is greatly reduced, letting the cook enjoy more of the cruise away from the galley. The convenience of turning on a burner and lighting it, as insignificant as it may seem, can be a major difference between cruising that is just camping, and cruising that is a genuine pleasure.

A STOVE RAIL FOR THE GALLEY

No matter how efficient your stove is, preparing a meal underway can be a tiring and dangerous task, especially on the smaller boat. Whether your stove is gimballed or fixed, it is not always easy for the cook to hang on, and rough seas and gusty winds can make matters worse.

Many boats have overhead handrails in the main cabin, but the area around the galley has nothing secure enough to get a good grip on. A rail in front of the stove and padeyes for the attachment of a safety belt for the cook should be considered necessities. A safety belt will keep the cook from falling away from the galley, but it will not keep him or her from falling forward, perhaps into a hot stove. This is the purpose of the rail across the front of the stove.

The first part of the job of installing a stove rail is to choose the components. While lighter material might be adequate, you can be sure that the rail will be sufficiently strong by using 1-inch, thick-walled stainless steel tubing—the type used for lifeline

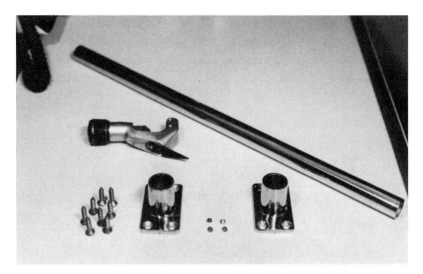

The components of stove rail installation: stainless steel tubing, tubing cutter, stanchion bases, set screws, and fasteners. Through-bolts should be used if possible.

stanchions. If the stove well is deep enough, the rail can be mounted on the inside faces of the well. This is perhaps the simplest installation, since it allows you to use conventional round or rectangular stanchion bases to secure the ends of the tubing.

If there isn't room inside the stove well to mount the rail, you can usually mount it outside the well on the face of the galley cabinets. You might have to use a little imagination, using 90-degree handrail fittings or even having the tubing bent at the ends. Bending will probably have to be done by a professional, since thick-walled stainless tubing is too stiff to bend with most manual tubing benders.

For a rail mounted inside the stove well, the installation is easy. Cut the tubing 1/2 inch shorter than the space to be spanned with either a tubing cutter or a hacksaw. If you use a hacksaw, dress the ends of the tubing smooth with a file after cutting, and clean off any loose filings thoroughly. Otherwise, you will get rust on the end of the tubing.

Back out the set screws in the bases and slide them over the ends of the tubing. The assembly can then be fitted into the space. Level it by installing one base with a single screw, then moving

The installed stove rail with the rectangular stanchion base secured to the face of the galley counter.

the other vertically until the assembly is level. Then secure the other base to the inside of the well.

The stanchion bases can be attached with large stainless steel screws, but through-bolting would be preferable if the area behind the bases is accessible. If the bases are mounted on the face of the galley rather than inside the well, through bolts are imperative, as the load on the fastenings is pure tension, and screws are weakest in tension.

* * *

Perhaps the trickiest part of the job is positioning the rail so it does not interfere with the operation of the stove. It should not block access to the control knobs, nor should it make it impossible to open the oven when the boat is heeled. Every installation will be different in this respect, so careful planning is required.

For twenty or thirty dollars and an hour of work, it would be difficult to beat this project for practicality and safety.

INSTALL A TEAK CABIN SOLE

What winter project could make a boat's cabin more attractive than the addition of a teak or teak and holly sole?

For upgrading a fiberglass or carpeted plywood cabin sole, you have two reasonable choices: You can use plywood made with strips of teak veneer interlaminated with narrow strips of holly veneer, or you can install individual teak strips with or without strips of holly.

The teak and holly veneer plywood is available from many marine lumber dealers in a 1/4-inch sheet. The plywood is cut to carefully fitted patterns, and can be laid in large sections, which are then trimmed with pieces of solid teak. The primary drawback to the teak and holly plywood is that the veneer is so thin that it must be well protected with varnish. Even varnished, it still remains vulnerable to damage from wear and anything dropped on it.

On the other hand, teak strips roughly 1-3/4 inches wide by 1/4 to 1/2 inch thick can be oiled and are virtually indestructible. Laying them is time-consuming compared with veneer plywood, but that is offset somewhat by the fact that no critically fashioned patterns are required.

A solid teak cabin sole is good looking, offers good footing, and looks great if kept scrubbed clean. But if you really want to be yachty, the way to go is with a sole of teak strips inlaid with strips of holly. This will cost a little more than a plain teak sole, and will be a bit more work. To look right, you must insure that the holly strips line up from one end of the cabin sole to the other. This requires careful fitting and planning, and results in more waste than a simple plain teak sole.

Teak is easy to find, but holly could present a problem. Chances are 99 out of 100 that your local lumber yard won't have it. Even many wholesale dealers specializing in hardwoods do not stock holly, as there is little demand for it. The holly tree is small, so there is not much usable lumber in a tree. Hunting down holly means checking in the yellow pages of the phone book under "hardwoods."

The primary domestic sources of holly are the south central

The sheathing covers the horizontal areas of the cabin sole and is cut and fitted where the sole meets the other cabinetry or the inside of the hull. The mitered strips around the sole openings and hatch edges are not essential, but provide a satisfying touch.

states, notably Arkansas and Oklahoma. According to Keiver-Willard Lumber Corporation, a major New England supplier of hardwoods, most of the holly they sell goes for boat work. The wholesale price for 4/4 holly is about $3.50 per board foot—less than teak, but more than Honduras mahogany or native walnut. Fortunately, you don't need much to do a cabin sole.

Holly is used in cabin soles for several reasons. First, it is almost pure white, contrasting nicely with teak. Second, unlike many light hardwoods such as ash and oak, it does not permanently stain black when it gets wet, so it is not necessary to varnish a teak and holly sole.

The easiest way to lay a teak and holly sole is to buy precut teak decking strips, which are 1/2 inch thick and about 2 inches wide. These strips have a rabbet approximately 1/4 inch by 1/4 inch cut along one edge of the strip. When used above decks,

The teak and holly cabin sole is the epitome of yachtiness.

the rabbet is filled with black caulking compound, and you end up with a deck that looks just like a laid and caulked deck. Teak decking strips are available from most major marine hardwood suppliers for about $.80 per lineal foot, which comes to about $4.80 per square foot.

For a cabin sole, simply rip and resaw the holly into strips to fit into the rabbet. When you glue down the teak to your existing cabin sole, glue the holly strips into the rabbet along each edge of the decking at the same time. If the holly strips are cut just the right size for the rabbet in the teak flooring, a little glue will hold them in position without requiring any pressure while the adhesive hardens.

If you have a fiberglass cabin sole, prepare the surface for bonding by rough-sanding the fiberglass surface. To follow the curvature of the hull where the sole meets the topsides or other joinerwork, mark each strip of teak roughly to shape, cut it out with a saber saw, and then plane it to the final shape. Cut and trim three or four strips at a time and then glue them all at once with thickened epoxy resin. With relatively thin decking (1/4 or 5/16 inch), you can probably weigh the strips down with chunks of scrap iron or plastic bags of sand. With 1/2-inch decking, you may have to screw it down to the existing cabin sole in order to eliminate voids in the adhesive. Stainless steel self-tapping sheet metal screws are then used to hold the teak in place as the glue cures. These can either be left in place and bunged after the glue has cured, or they can be removed and the holes left behind counterbored and plugged. After the glue sets up, plane or sand down any high ridges of the holly or globs of epoxy resin that have squeezed out between the strips of wood.

Is a teak and holly sole unnecessary? Perhaps. Does installing one involve a good deal of work? Certainly. Are the results elegant? Absolutely.

MAKE YOU OWN
COMPANIONWAY HATCH SCREENS

Warm weather cruising brings with it the need for flow-through ventilation to make sleeping possible. Unfortunately, open hatches also invite mosquitoes below. Velcro screen kits are a quick and easy solution to this problem, but wood-framed screens look much nicer and are much more versatile.

Built as one-for-one replacements for the drop boards, hatch screens can be used in combination with the drop boards to vary the size of the screened opening according to the weather. Also, if the top screen has a hasp identical to the one on the top drop board, you can leave your boat reasonably secure but well ventilated while the crew is ashore sightseeing or shopping.

Each screen consists of an outer and inner frame with the fiberglass screening held between them. The frame should be of the same thickness as the drop boards and of stock wide enough so that screen tension will not cause bowing (about 1-1/4 inches to 1-1/2 inches should be adequate).

To build the screens, start by cutting the sides of the outer frame to the exact length of the corresponding side of the drop board. Next make the corner joints. Any type corner joint which is strong enough will do. We prefer the mitered lap joint because

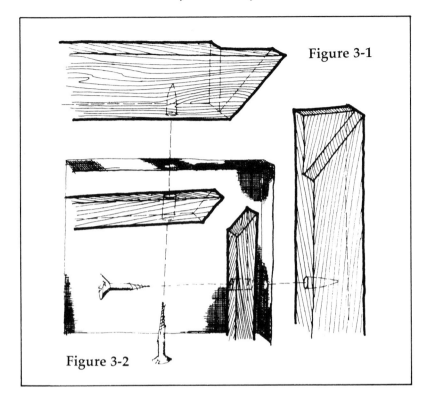

Figure 3-1

Figure 3-2

it looks good while providing a large enough gluing surface for strength (**Figure 3-1**). To make the first half of this joint, make a 45-degree cut half way through the thickness and carefully trim away the waste with a chisel. A good-looking joint requires a careful fit, but the use of epoxy glue will allow slight imperfections without a loss in strength.

The second half of the joint is a little more complicated. Two miter cuts are required. Make the first cut at 45 degrees all the way through the stock. Make the second cut at 90 degrees half way through at exactly the lower end of the 45 degree cut as shown in **Figure 3-2**. After you make both cuts, trim away the waste with the chisel. Now hold the joint halves together in the assembled position to check for fit. Carefully shave either or both halves of the joint to get a good fit. With a pencil, mark numbers on both halves of the joint so that you can join the same halves when gluing. If all this seems a little too complicated, a simple half-lap joint, a splined miter, or a doweled butt joint will certainly suffice.

When you have all four corner joints cut, begin gluing by applying a liberal coat of epoxy on each surface to be joined. Then assemble the frame on a table top protected by waxed paper. After checking for squareness, put waxed paper on the top of each corner and weigh it down. You must be careful not to shift the frame out of square when placing the weights on it. Recheck the squareness after the weights are in place, then make any minor corrections necessary.

Now you are ready to cut the inner frame sides. Make them from square stock, the same thickness as the outer frame. The corners are simple 45-degree miter joints. Do not glue these joints. Glued corners will not allow the slight expansion necessary to pinch the screening between the inner and outer frames. A neat job depends on a good snug fit of the inner frame within the outer frame. Otherwise the unglued corner joints of the inner frame will open up too much.

Next bore the screw holes using a combination countersink bit. Clamp each inner frame side to the outer frame to be sure the same alignment is held during the entire operation. Three screws, evenly spaced, should be enough for the short sides, with five for the long sides. The screws at each end should be as close to the corners as drill clearance will permit. Matching inner and outer frame sides should be marked to ensure that the holes line up during final assembly.

Cut the fiberglass screening about two inches oversize all the way around. Then lay the outer frame over it and locate the exact points of the inner corners of the frame on the screening. Cut a 90-degree notch in the screen at each corner point. Do any finish sanding necessary and you are ready for the final assembly.

Lay the outer frame down on a flat surface and lay the screening over it. Make sure the corner notches in the screen line up with the frame corners. Holding the outer frame and screening in alignment (an assistant is useful at this point), push the inner frame sides down within the outer frame so that each side of the screening bends up and is caught between the inner and outer frames. The inner frame corners may need trimming in the miter box to allow for the thickness of the screening, but be careful to retain a snug fit. Next, drive the screws in far enough to bind the screening slightly. This will allow you to add tension to the screening by grasping the excess screening between the thumb and forefinger and pulling while tightening the adjacent screws. Be careful not to distort the screening while doing this. The weave in the screening should be straight and parallel with the frame sides when you are finished. You may need to loosen some of the screws to adjust the tension and then retighten them. Finally, trim the excess screening away with a sharp knife.

As a final note, you might prefer to counterbore the screw holes and use wood plugs to cover the screw heads. If the screws are driven carefully and the slots lined up parallel to the frame, however, the countersunk screw heads will not look objectionable. This will also make disassembly of the screens easier for varnishing or replacement of the screening if necessary.

A DO-IT-YOURSELF "UNVENTILATOR"

Everyone knows that getting enough fresh air into a boat can be a problem. But what do you do if there is too much fresh air? For most boatowners, the answer is to stuff a towel into the vent tubes from the dorade boxes. Here, however, is a neater way to do it, courtesy of Hinckley & Company.

A disk slightly larger in diameter than the vent tube opening to be covered is cut from any thin plastic, such as PVC or acrylic. If the top of the dorade box is translucent, use translucent plastic so light will still get below. If the hole through the deck is 4 inches, for example, make the plastic disk 4-1/4 inches in diameter. Cut an oval frame from solid lumber or high-grade plywood that matches the other interior wood in the boat. The wood should be about twice as thick as the plastic disk.

A rabbet must be cut in the underside of the oval frame, as deep as the plastic disk, and wide enough to accommodate the disk with just a little play. The rabbet is best cut with a rabbeting bit in a router. For a handle, a small drawer pull can be installed in the center of the disk by simply drilling through the disk and screwing it in place.

To install the unventilator, drop the disk into the rabbet in the

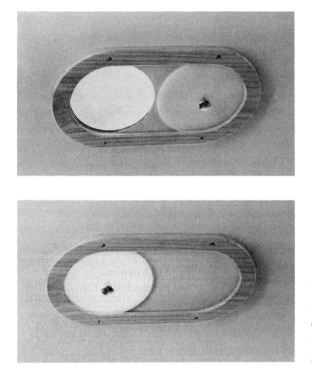

The "unventilator" is shown open above, and closed in the bottom photo.

frame, then screw the frame to the cabin overhead using counter-sunk oval-head screws. When shut, the disk will cut out almost all the air flow through the dorade vent. In addition, if the disk fits tightly against the overhead, it will keep water from coming below in heavy weather.

SHEATHING PLYWOOD BULKHEADS

Back in the early days of fiberglass boatbuilding, a nameless marketing man decided that the key to selling a boat built of the otherwise undistinguished new material was to stress the idea that fiberglass boats were completely maintenance free. No more painting. No more varnishing. No more rot. Fiberglass everything. In carrying this idea to its absurd conclusion, some-one decided that wood on the interior of boats had to go, too.

To preserve a feeling of wood down below, someone de-cided to cover the exposed surfaces belowdecks with a hideous material: laminated plastic designed to look like wood. This was the beginning of the First Dark Age in modern boat design.

A few years later, another marketing man—the same one, for all we know—concluded that fake wood looked just a little too cheap and cold. What was needed below was some real wood. Instead of plastic bulkheads, we got bulkheads of varnished mahogany plywood.

Then, as the industry started to grow and competition got hotter, some builder, looking for a way to save money, realized that there were dozens of man-hours involved in varnishing those bulkheads. In a moment of inspiration, he reasoned that most of those hours could be saved if he did not have to varnish all those surfaces.

Mahogany must be varnished, not only to look good but also to have reasonable weather resistance. Being a resourceful boatbuilder, he decided that he would use bulkheads of teak plywood, which would look expensive and could simply be treated with a coat of oil to provide some luster to what is otherwise a pretty dull wood. He killed two birds with one stone. He knocked dozens of hours (and therefore hundreds of dollars) off the cost of his boats, while still retaining the look of wood below—expensive wood, at that. The Second Dark Age of boatbuilding was upon us.

Except for those who can afford the products of some enlightened builders—usually builders of custom or semicustom boats—boatowners still dwell in those dark teak caves. But a new age is upon us. Instead of dark teak interiors, we are beginning to see boats with ceilings, trim, and even entire bulkheads of lighter woods such as ash and cedar.

The use of light-colored woods below is very traditional. Classic Concordia yawls had interiors either of knotty pine or knot-free locust. Herreshoff and Lawley used butternut—a member of the walnut family—to keep interiors light in weight and color. If you are tired of the teak cave look, you can modernize (or classicize, if you prefer to think of it that way) your boat's interior by resurfacing those teak surfaces with other woods.

Be forewarned: This is neither an easy project nor a cheap one. It requires careful planning, meticulous workmanship, and a good eye for balancing color. It also requires access to some

A light-colored hardwood sheathing can turn a simple plywood bulkhead into a thing of beauty.

fairly sophisticated woodworking machinery, or the willingness to pay for someone else's time to do the millwork for you.

Choosing Wood

Teak is at its best underfoot, where left bare it provides good traction. Teak is excellent for both interior and exterior trim, because trim is constantly getting bumped and dinged, or having its finish worn off. Teak is almost unique among woods in that it suffers very little from having the bare wood surface exposed to the elements. Teak trim which gets gouged or scratched can be revarnished without bleaching or scraping, usually with only minimal sanding. Even badly abused teak left unvarnished outside for years can be brought back to its original color with chemical cleaning. Mahogany, oak, ash, butternut—almost any other wood, in fact—will permanently discolor if left exposed to the elements for long.

But teak is a dark wood, heavy in both appearance and weight. Granted, the half millimeter veneer on teak plywood adds little or nothing to the weight of the boat, but the visual weight can be overwhelming, particularly if not offset by large masses of white or other light colors.

Ash and oak are light in color, heavy in weight. They also have the bad habit of turning black when in contact with moisture, and moisture is everywhere in a boat. To keep maintenance of these woods to a minimum, they should not be used where exposed to wear or weather (trim inside a hatch, cabins soles, or galley countertops, for example). Being extremely hard, working with both ash and oak requires professional quality tools, such as carbide saw blades and router bits. Plain steel saw blades are quickly dulled by hardwoods.

Mahogany is a traditional wood both below and above decks. Stained and varnished, it may be as dark as, or darker than teak, and therefore may not significantly lighten the interior of a boat. Only real Honduras mahogany—almost salmon pink before varnishing—looks good when varnished without stain.

Other woods suitable for belowdecks use include various cedars, pines, birch, locust, cherry, and butternut. All of these are suitable for lamination over existing teak plywood bulkheads. The choice depends on taste as much as anything else.

A word of caution: Softwoods such as cedar are susceptible to damage from bumping. The surface of these woods becomes substantially harder with the buildup of numerous coats of varnish, but never gets hard enough to make them suitable for roughly treated items such as door or drawer trim, table tops, or other surfaces subject to physical abuse. A great deal of care is required when building things from softwoods to keep from marring the wood while you are working. On the plus side, the softer woods sand very easily, so that flaws and dings are more easily removed.

Matchboard

The ideal form of lumber for sheathing plywood bulkheads is what is known as matchboard. Unless you are an experienced woodworker, you probably call the matchboard "tongue and groove" stock, for it consists of thin, narrow stock with a tongue milled along one edge and a groove milled along the other. The edge of each side of each piece is chamfered at a slight angle. The boards fit together neatly, or "match." The chamfered edges provide definition between each plank, giving a matchboard surface its distinctive appearance. In addition, slight variations in grain, texture, and color give the strakes of a matchboard bulkhead an interesting appearance that is "unmatched" by a seamless teak veneer peeled off a log by a huge lathe.

In practice, a useful alternative to matchboard is what might be considered "fake matchboard," since the stock used in sheathing a plywood bulkhead is too thin to mill a true tongue and groove along each edge. Instead, in section it looks like a piece of matchboard that has been sliced in half horizontally, producing two pieces of wood, each a little less than half the thickness of the original (**Figure 3-3**). The reasons for doing this are simple: to reduce weight, and to save material. If you think this halved matchboard looks familiar in section, it is called shiplapping, and was used to make structural ceilings on the inside of wooden hulls (albeit with much thicker planking).

Full thickness matchboard used in house or boat construction is nominally one inch thick, and usually about 3/4 inch finished. You can make solid bulkheads of material this thickness, as was common in the days of wooden boats. But all you want to do in this case is cover an existing surface; the additional wood you add need not contribute strength to the bulkhead, so it should be made as thin as is practical.

Do not use veneers, which are usually 1/8 inch thick or less. They are too thin to saw easily, and cannot take the chamfered edge between pieces that gives a matchboard bulkhead much of its character. Veneers are also hard to glue to a vertical surface without vacuum bagging, which is more trouble than it is worth for a project of this type.

Sheathing a plywood bulkhead is most practical in new construction, before the complications of other joinerwork are attached to the bulkhead. In an existing boat, some interior disassembly might have to be done, but a careful craftsman can do the job with careful fitting around the existing joinerwork.

Additional Considerations

Before you decide to sheath bulkheads in hardwood, you must first determine if the process is practical at all. If the job is to look as if it were part of the original construction, the door and corner trim will probably have to be removed from the bulkhead, and new trim fabricated to match the additional thickness of the

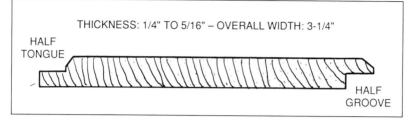

THICKNESS: 1/4" TO 5/16" – OVERALL WIDTH: 3-1/4"

HALF TONGUE

HALF GROOVE

Figure 3-3. A Section of Bulkhead Sheathing

bulkhead. This will be necessary unless the original trim sticks out past the surface of the bulkhead by 3/8 inch or more, in which case you can get away with fitting right up to the original trim. Be forewarned that ready-made trim available from wood-products companies such as H&L Woodwork are sized for bulkheads of standard thicknesses, such as 1/2 inch and 3/4 inch. Your sheathed bulkheads are likely to be of an odd thickness, and may therefore require you to make custom trim.

The second problem is fitting around existing joinerwork or other parts of the boat's structure. Some boats have molded recesses in a hull liner into which the bulkheads are fitted. Can you work up to these with a surface that is at least 1/4 inch thicker than the original without it looking odd? Can you easily fit the sheathing around longitudinal components that meet the bulkhead at right angles, such as the faces and backs of settees?

Fitting the bulkhead sheathing is not a difficult process; in fact, it is far easier to fit narrow pieces of matchboard than it is to install an entire plywood bulkhead. Nevertheless, the job does require patience and careful planning.

Buying Wood

If the project looks feasible, the next step is to purchase the wood. Don't overlook the local lumberyard. There are a number of ready-made tongue and groove products that might be usable. You might find that you can buy matchboard or a similar thin hardwood paneling at the local lumberyard for less than the cost of making it from rough lumber.

Matchboard of 1x4-inch nominal dimension finishes at about 3/4 inch by 3-1/2 inches, almost ideal for resawing to make bulkhead sheathing. If you can find matchboard in this dimension of a material you like, you are in business. If not, you will have to buy rough lumber, then either mill it yourself or contract with a millwork shop to do the work. Unless you are set up for it, a millwork shop is likely to be able to do the job more quickly and efficiently than you can, and may also be able to purchase the rough stock at better prices than you can.

Calculate the amount of wood you will need by figuring the area in square feet to be covered, and then converting that to a linear measure of boards the size you will use. For example, if your bulkheads total 100 square feet, and each piece of stock covers a 3-inch-wide section of bulkhead, you will need 400 linear feet of finished stock. Allow at least 10 percent for waste, offcuts, and flaws in pieces that render them useless.

Lumber that starts off 3/4 inch thick can be resawn to give two boards about 5/16 inch thick. This is not a bad thickness to work with, and it means that for 440 linear feet of finished stock, you would need to start out with 220 linear feet of full thickness 1x4-inch stock. If you are working from rough lumber one inch thick (4/4, in lumber industry parlance) that would translate to about 75 board feet of lumber, assuming it can be purchased in widths that minimize waste.

To a large extent, the type of wood determines the amount of waste material. Mahogany comes from huge trees, and is usually fairly free of knots. There is also little waste in Alaskan yellow cedar, western red cedar, redwood, and Douglas fir. Woods that come from trees with small trunks or lots of low branches, such as butternut and eastern white cedar, usually have large knots and other flaws that mean a lot of waste if you want perfectly clear material.

Millwork

Figure 3-3 shows the ideal dimensions for bulkhead sheathing, although the thickness can be adjusted slightly if you wish. Material thinner than 1/4 inch is hard to handle and glue down. Material thicker than 5/16 inch is unnecessarily heavy, but may be required if you are attempting to hide bulkhead tabbing. In this case, the thick stock can be relieved (cut away on the face next to the bulkhead) to fit neatly over the tabbing.

Jigs used on the table saw can make complicated millwork jobs safer.

If you have purchased ready-made matchboard that needs to be resawn, you can do it yourself on a band saw or heavy-duty 10-inch table saw. If you use a table saw, use a 20- to 40-tooth carbide combination blade or ripping blade with as narrow a kerf as you can find. Carefully set up the fence to rip each board exactly in the middle, so that you split the tongue and groove. It is important to try to retain as much of the tongue as possible, since it serves as part of the fastening system, as you will see later.

One of the most important parts of any millwork is creating jigs for your saw that allow you full control of the work while keeping your hands away from the blade. If you have no experience with this, standard woodworking references such as Roger Cliffe's *Table Saw Techniques* (Sterling Publishing Company, New York, 1984) contain information on constructing jigs of various types. A series of featherboards clamped to your saw's rip fence and table will hold the work down and in place.

The proper tools to make the bulkhead sheathing from rough lumber include a table saw with normal blades and a dado set, a jointer for truing up boards before final sawing, and a thickness planer to finish and dimension the lumber. A shaper, or router mounted under a workbench, can also speed things up. Unless you already have the proper tools, however, the simplest choice is to contract with a millwork shop to do the job.

From rough boards to finished stock should take a good shop about four to five hours to make your 440 feet of material—perhaps $120 to $150 in labor costs in a small shop, or about 30 cents per linear foot over and above the cost of the material. If you use 75 board feet of lumber that costs $2.50 per board foot, you have spent about $190 on raw material, or about $300 to $350 for wood for the whole project. Not cheap, as we said!

Whether you make your sheathing stock from matchboard or rough lumber, once you finish the resawing, surface plane the resawn side of each board to remove the inevitable saw blade marks. If you are milling your sheathing from rough-cut lumber, the next step is to cut the rabbet which will simulate the tongue and groove in each edge of the boards. This can be done on a table saw blade, or with a rabbeting bit in a router or shaper, depending on the tools you have available.

Don't be tempted to avoid the rabbeting step and simply chamfer the edges of the square-edged stock. When you are gluing the sheathing down, glue will ooze through the joint between planks, making it almost impossible to keep the V-groove between planks clean and sharp.

The last step in making the stock is to chamfer each of the two edges on the face. This can be done with a chamfering bit in a router or shaper, or on the table saw, with the blade set at a 45-degree angle. A little trial and error will show you the proper setting for the blade, and the proper positioning of the rip fence.

Undoubtedly, some of your pieces of sheathing will have flaws in them—poor grain, poor color, or knots. As much as possible, you should try to work around these flaws. With a little planning, you can hide most of the flaws in locations that will not show when the job is finished, such as behind book racks or settee cushions. That is one reason for making extra sheathing stock: The inevitable badly flawed pieces can go unused.

Fastening the Sheathing
Prepare the plywood bulkhead surface for sheathing by power sanding with coarse (60 grit) sandpaper. If the bulkhead is teak

plywood, follow this up with an alcohol wipedown to remove surface oils just before gluing down the sheathing.

The tongue part of your sheathing stock has two purposes: to keep the joint between pieces of sheathing from oozing glue, and to assist in positioning and fastening the stock to the bulkhead. The bulkhead sheathing is attached using a combination of mechanical fasteners and adhesive. Epoxy resin, thickened slightly with a material similar in color to the sheathing (such as fine sawdust from making the stock, or a commercial thickener such as WEST System® Tan Filleting Blend) provides the primary holding power. Staples can be used as mechanical fasteners and to hold the sheathing in position while the glue sets, but add little to the structural integrity of the installation. We recommend using an Arrow T-50 tacker with 3/8-inch Monel staples.

You should not use screws to fasten the sheathing, except in areas where they are required to get the sheathing to lay down flat. Even carefully matched bungs in screw holes will detract slightly from the appearance of the finished bulkhead.

Fitting

The first piece of sheathing installed is the most critical. It must be absolutely plumb, since the sheathing consists of a series of vertical lines which will not look right if they do not line up with other verticals in the boat. Beginning next to a doorway or other true vertical allows you to clamp the first piece into position before gluing, so you can line it up carefully. It is best to overlap the doorway slightly with the first piece, since a joint in the sheathing which lines up with the edge of the doorway will look odd. You can trim off the overlap with a router or saber saw after the bulkhead is sheathed.

The tongue edge of each piece of stock is the working edge— the edge against which the next piece will be fitted. If you try to do it the other way around, you will not be able to staple each piece into position.

An adjustable bevel gauge can be used to take off the angles where the sheathing meets the cabin top or other joinery. In some areas, a cardboard template may be more useful; it is better to make a mistake in cutting a piece of cardboard than a piece of expensive wood. You can make minor adjustments in the fit of sheathing with a sanding block wrapped with coarse sandpaper. The sanding block allows subtle shaping of the top to conform with the camber of the cabintop, and is less likely to cause splinters than using a tool such as a block plane.

When you are satisfied with the position of the first piece of sheathing, clamp it firmly in place on the bulkhead. Strike a pencil line on the bulkhead along the working edge of the sheathing as an alignment reference. Fit the second piece in the same fashion as the first, once again using clamps to hold it in position after fitting. From here on out, you will not be able to directly clamp pieces in position. Instead, clamp a batten to the bulkhead long enough to reach over the piece of sheathing currently being fitted. A thin wedge under the batten will apply enough pressure to the sheathing to keep it from sliding out of place as you work.

We have found it best to install no more than four pieces of sheathing—about a foot of bulkhead width—in any one gluing. More than that becomes awkward to glue, clamp, and staple in place. It is better to cover the bulkhead a little bit at a time, than to try to save time by doing it all at once.

After the last piece of sheathing for the first gluing is dry fitted, strike another pencil line on the bulkhead along the working edge of this piece. This will indicate the edge of the section of bulkhead to be painted with adhesive for the first gluing. Number the pieces before removing them from the bulkhead, either writing the numbers on masking tape stuck to the surface or by lightly pencilling numbers on each face.

Gluing

Since epoxy resin has a short pot life, get everything ready before mixing up the glue. Lay the pieces of sheathing on a table covered with polyethylene sheeting, and use a foam brush or foam roller to coat both the back of the sheathing and the face of the bulkhead with unfilled resin. Then mix some thickener into the resin and brush another coat onto the back of each piece of sheathing. The thickened resin should be the consistency of honey, so it will fill any gaps between the sheathing and the bulkhead surface. It should be brushed out fairly evenly, leveling with a wide putty knife if necessary.

Thin wedges under the battens can be used to apply local pressure to the edge of each piece of sheathing.

Be careful to line up the first piece of sheathing with the line you drew on the bulkhead as a reference mark. Use C-clamps to hold it in position, and then staple the tongue to the bulkhead, using firm pressure on the tacker to drive the staples in as far as possible. The staples should be placed about a foot apart, as far in from the edge of the tongue as possible, with the long axis of the staple parallel to the edge of the tongue. Even using a lot of pressure on the tacker, the staples will probably not drive all the way into the bulkhead. Use a 1/4-inch-diameter pin punch and a hammer to set them flush with the surface of the tongue.

Aligning the next piece is easier, since it is simply butted up against the edge of the first piece, then stapled down. After stapling the edge of the second piece, you will notice that its groove edge—which is not stapled down—has probably lifted slightly, and is not lying down flush. This edge, and the corresponding edge in the next pieces, will be wedged down after all the pieces in a single gluing are stapled in place on the bulkhead.

Now you see why it is best to fit only a few pieces of sheathing at a time.

After you attach the next pieces in the same manner, you must now make the sheathing lie down flat. This is done with a number of wooden battens about 3/4 inch square. Clamp one end of each of the battens to the edge of the bulkhead, allowing the other ends to overlap the last piece of sheathing by a couple of inches. Drive a screw through the end of each batten into the bulkhead, just past the last piece of sheathing. The screw hole in the bulkhead will be covered by the sheathing applied later.

While the batten will do a pretty good job of flattening out the sheathing, you will probably have to use thin wedges or shims under the batten to really hold things down flat. By pressing on the face of the sheathing with your fingers, you will be able to feel any sections that are not lying down flat on the bulkhead below. Add more battens and wedges as necessary to hold each piece down firmly.

Now, using a rag dipped in stove alcohol or shellac thinner, clean up the glue that has squeezed out between the pieces of sheathing. Use a putty knife to clean any epoxy from the beveled groove between the strakes, as it is difficult to remove once it cures. Also use the putty knife to clean up any glue that has squeeze past the edge of the last piece of sheathing. This will leave the bulkhead clean for the fitting and gluing of the next group of pieces.

Successive fittings and gluings generally get easier, although your hold-down battens must get longer and longer as you proceed. A few screws through the sheathing itself may be inevitable, as it will undoubtedly be impossible to wedge some pieces completely flat on a large bulkhead. Use as few fastenings as possible, and make them fairly large-diameter panhead self-tappers driven only flush with the surface. After the glue cures, the fasteners can be removed and the screw holes counterbored and bunged with plugs cut from the sheathing material.

Work from roughly the centerline of the bulkhead all the way to one side, then work from the center to the other side. You will have to reverse the direction the tongue of the sheathing points when you begin working from the center toward the opposite side, since the tongue would otherwise be hidden. Do this by first

Careful fitting is required where the sheathing butts against other joiner-work, the hull sides, or the cabintop.

gluing a thin "tongue" under the grooved edge of the first piece of sheathing you installed. You are now ready to start gluing in the other direction.

Finishing

With an orbital sander, begin the finishing with coarse paper, gradually working from 50 or 60 grit down to about 100 grit. You can use a block plane to cut down any badly raised edges which were not wedged completely down. Don't worry about them coming loose. Some voids behind the sheathing are inevitable, but they will not affect anything.

After machine sanding, you must do the finish sanding by hand. Go back to 80-grit paper, sanding with the grain. Sand out any machine sander swirls on the surface with 80-grit paper before moving on to 100, then 120 grit. On straight-grained wood you can stop with 120 grit, but highly-figured wood must be further sanded with 150 and 180 grit to remove fine scratches.

We prefer a satin finish on interior woodwork. It hides flaws better than gloss varnish, and looks more like a traditional hand-

The finished product: long-lasting beauty replaces a dull plywood bulkhead.

rubbed finish. If you are a real purist, you can varnish with gloss varnish until the grain of the wood is completely filled; then rub down the surface with powdered pumice on a cloth dampened with water or furniture oil.

Hand rubbing will eventually produce a beautiful surface, but at the cost of untold hours of labor. For most of us, a satin interior varnish is a more than reasonable substitute. Use at least five coats to fill the grain. Sand between each coat with 180-grit paper, using a tack rag to clean the surface just before applying the next coat of varnish.

*   *   *

In new construction, the edges of bulkheads are covered with a margin piece to hide any fitting errors or rough edges. The margin pieces should be of either the same wood as the bulkhead, or of a contrasting wood. The margin pieces should be fairly thin, and must be carefully fitted to the side of the hull. If a ceiling is to be installed, margin pieces may be unnecessary.

In sheathing the bulkheads in an existing boat, either reuse the original margin pieces, or make new ones of the same material as your new bulkhead, using the old pieces as patterns. The margin pieces should not be glued; simply screw them on with counterbored and bunged flat-head screws or with countersunk oval-head screws.

Sheathing bulkheads is not a simple project, nor is it beyond the scope of the amateur woodworker. With careful planning and cautious execution, hardwood-sheathed bulkheads can give your boat an interior unmatched by veneer plywood.

PLASTIC LAMINATE
FOR INTERIOR JOINERY PROJECTS

The ability to work with plastic laminate is extremely handy to have in your bag of tricks if you are upgrading or rebuilding a cruising boat. Many do-it-yourselfers seem to shy away from this material for fear that it is expensive, the techniques are difficult to master, or that a large inventory of tools and machinery is required. All of these concerns, however, are unwarranted.

Before we go any farther, we should point out that although we occasionally use the brand name *Formica* in place of the generic term "plastic laminate." There are many manufacturers of plastic laminate, and very little difference, it seems, in the quality of the material.

Plastic laminate is made of several layers of resin-saturated paper, laminated together under heat and pressure, with the top layer of paper being the color of the finished surface. In the case of laminates with a "wood-grain" or "marble" surface, the top layer of paper is actually offset printed with a photograph of a wood or marble surface.

We believe that the smooth, uniformly colored surface of Formica has an aesthetic appeal all its own. As we have already mentioned, however, we do not believe that this appeal extends to the wood-grain laminates. It seems to us that if you want a wood-veneer surface on a bulkhead or a berth riser, then wood veneer or veneer plywood is the material to use, rather than a plastic-coated photograph of a piece of wood veneer. This opinion applies equally to plastic-coated pictures of pieces of marble.

Traditionally, the yacht interior was painted with white or a light pastel semigloss or "eggshell" enamel, and trimmed with varnished or oiled hardwood of a contrasting color. The currently fashionable "Taiwanese-style," all-wood interior can be dark, "close," and downright depressing after a few days or weeks at sea. The use of light, solid-colored plastic laminates on bulkheads and other large surfaces can produce a bright, cheerful yacht interior without the initial effort or the upkeep of paint. Paint, of course, requires careful surface preparation, and a build-up of several coats, with sanding in between. Formica, on the other hand, requires minimal surface preparation, produces a finish that will last for many years, and covers completely with "one coat."

Most of the whites, off-whites and light pastel-colored laminates are available in two finishes (glossy and "suede"), and in two thicknesses (1/16 inch and 1/32 inch). The matte or suede finish very closely approximates an eggshell enamel finish, and is generally the finish of choice for the traditional interior. There are a couple of problems with the use of the glossy material for yacht joinerwork. First, the glossy surfaced laminates tend to scratch easily, both in the shop and in use, and the glossy laminates tend to display those scratches prominently.

Second, glossy Formica looks very much like molded, gelcoated fiberglass—a look that many craftsmen attempt to avoid in the construction of a custom interior. Still, some of the glossy laminates do have a bold, striking appearance which can be used to advantage in "high-tech," or "European-style" interiors.

The 1/16-inch laminates should be used for horizontal working surfaces such as galley countertops, navigation and dining tables. The 1/32-inch material, often called "vertical surfacing," is intended for vertical surfaces (not surprisingly), like berth risers, bulkheads, cabinet fronts and doors. As 1/32-inch laminate is half the weight and about two-thirds the cost of the thicker material, it pays to use vertical surfacing wherever possible. In use, we have found that the thin material holds up very well on "low-traffic" horizontal surfaces such as bookshelves, dresser and vanity tops; but to stand up for any length of time to the shuffling of pots, pans, bottles, and blocks of ice; the thicker material is necessary.

Other adhesives are sometimes used for wood and plastic veneer in high volume manufacturing plants, but solvent-based contact cement is the only adhesive practical for use by the home craftsman. Contact cement is waterproof (or at least highly water-resistant), but it does soften given sufficient heat and it is not solvent-resistant. For this reason, furniture-grade veneers and plastic laminates are best suited for use below decks, where they are for the most part out of direct contact with the heat of the sun. This does not mean that you can not use a veneer or laminate-covered table for dining in the cockpit, but for permanent installations on deck, these materials are not suitable.

Color Selection

The smaller the boat, the more it will benefit from an interior as light, open, and "airy" as possible. Although an interior sheathed in a light-colored wood will seem larger and more open than one paneled in teak or mahogany, the cabin will still be darker and feel smaller than one finished in a light-colored paint or plastic laminate. The illusion of space is not so much a characteristic of the color's "value," but of the "temperature" of the color. The earth-tone colors of all woods, even the lighter colored woods such as oak and ash, are still "warm" colors; and warm colors have a tendency to feel "close."

Cool colors, on the other hand—blues, greens, cool grays, and even some tints of pale lavender and pink—tend to recede from the eye. Perhaps more importantly, cool colors provide an interesting contrast with the warm colors of natural wood. Plastic laminates, in cool, pastel colors, provide an opportunity to make use of this "temperature" contrast; making an interior seem cooler, larger, and more cheerful. And believe it or not, cool colors can actually help to soothe jagged nerves when the wind outside is screaming through the rigging.

On a more practical side, Formica surfaces are easy to maintain, requiring only an occasional squirt of *Fantastic* or *409* and a quick wipe with a damp cloth. Plastic laminate will not fade, and it resists dents, scratches, and stains; these surfaces will look as good after five years as they did when they were new.

Application Techniques

To illustrate the tools and techniques used for applying and finishing plastic laminate, we have chosen to show the construction of a vanity top to be installed in the head of a 37-foot cutter. It is a simple project, but it requires all of the basic laminating

A router is used to trim the excess from the first piece of laminate installed, the self-edge at the front of the counter.

techniques.

To keep the weight at a minimum, this top is made of 1/2-inch plywood (although a galley counter or bookshelf which must support a load might well be made of thicker ply). To stiffen the panel, and to increase the apparent thickness for aesthetic reasons, a buildup is often applied around the perimeter of a top—3/4-inch fir in this case. We frequently use plastic resin glue and bronze staples for this type of non-structural joiner-work, but galvanized finish nails or screws and any type of waterproof adhesive is equally suitable.

Before proceeding with the application of the laminate, be sure that the surface to be covered is clean and sanded smooth. Formica will cover seams and joints in the substrate without difficulty, but gaping joints, knot holes and screw heads may later print through the plastic surface if they are not filled. Because it sets up quickly and sands easily (with a belt sander, at least), we usually use polyester autobody putty to fill any defects in the wood surface prior to applying the laminate.

The laminate can be cut with a circular saw or table saw, with tin snips, or with nibblers made especially for the purpose.

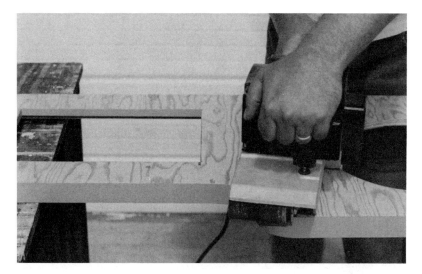

A belt sander is used to cut the laminate down flush with the plywood substrate prior to applying the plastic to the top surface. Note that laminate has also been applied to the inside edges of the hatch opening at the left.

Perhaps the best way, however, is simply to score the laminate deeply with a utility knife drawn against a metal straightedge; then break the laminate along the scored line. The pieces of laminate are always cut a little larger than the surfaces they are to cover. A quarter of an inch is plenty of extra width for a strip covering the edge of a door or the front of a countertop, as these small pieces are quite easy to handle. For a large surface, it is better to add an inch to the width and length of the substrate panel when cutting the laminate.

As mentioned earlier, solvent-based contact cement is used to adhere the laminate. For most small jobs, a throwaway bristle paint brush is the most practical means of applying the adhesive. One fairly thick coat of adhesive on both mating surfaces is usually sufficient, although two coats will not hurt, particularly on wood which tends to absorb a small amount of the cement. For larger jobs, special roller covers (with a carpet-like surface) are available from laminate dealers. We prefer to roll on the adhesive as the roller puts down more adhesive in less time, and gives more uniform coverage. After using one of these roller covers, incidentally, you need not wash it or throw it away. Just

When applying pressure to bond the laminate, be careful not to crack the plastic at the edges of the substrate panel.

roll out the excess adhesive on a piece of scrap and let the roller dry. When you go to use it again, the solvent in the fresh adhesive will dissolve the old adhesive in the roller cover and quickly soften it up.

The laminate is applied to one surface at a time, then once adhered, it is trimmed flush with the substrate panel. The tool of choice for this job is a flush-trimmer bit with a ball-bearing pilot wheel (sometimes called a laminate trimmer) mounted in a light-duty router.

Generally, it is best to do the edges of a panel first. In the case of the vanity top, since only the front edge and the top surface will show, the strip of laminate covering the front edge is applied first. To cover a hatch cover or a cabinet door, begin by laminating a strip on each of two opposite edges. (In case you are wondering, the square hatch shown in the photo of this top provides access to a laundry bin behind the head.)

After the laminate is trimmed flush using the router, the edges still need to be smoothed in order to produce a perfect seam with the next piece of laminate to be applied. An inexpensive belt sander is helpful for this job, although it can be done fairly easily with a metal file or a sanding block. For that matter,

Once the perimeter of the panel, the hatch opening, and the sink cutout have been trimmed with the router, the final job is dressing the edges with a file.

the router is also unnecessary, if you are willing to devote the time and elbow grease required to trimming with a file and a sanding block. Hand tools, in fact, are preferable for small edges and corners, as they are easier to handle. A 100-grit sanding belt, slipped over a snugly fitting wooden block, is helpful for this and many other small sanding jobs.

In the case of the hatch cover, we are now ready to apply strips of laminate to the other two edges, followed by pieces of laminate on the top and bottom surfaces. Since the front edge is the only one we are covering on the countertop itself, we can proceed with laminating the top surface. After the plastic is rough cut to shape and the contact cement has dried on both mating surfaces, position the laminate over the countertop. Use a few wooden sticks or dowels laid across the wood surface to keep the glued surfaces out of contact with each other until you are sure the Formica sheet is in the proper position. Once you are satisfied with the position of the plastic sheet, begin at one end, removing the sticks or dowels and applying hand pressure to smooth out and adhere the laminate.

Additional pressure needs to be applied to the plastic surface at this point to develop the full bond-strength of the adhesive.

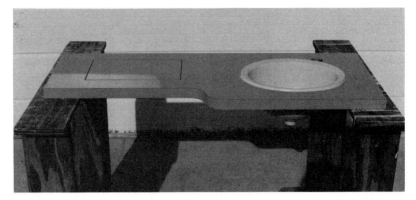

The finished top, less the hardware and fixtures, is now ready to install.

For thin strips on the edges of panels, work down the edge with a series of smart raps with a rubber mallet. For large surfaces, a J-roller (available from your laminate dealer) can be used to apply the needed pressure, or you can accomplish the same thing by moving a small block of wood around the surface, smacking the block with a hammer.

The top surface of the counter is now ready to be trimmed with the router, all around the outside edges. You can drill a hole through the laminate to get the bit started, and then use the router to trim around inside edges, such as the cutout for the sink and the laundry bin hatch.

Dressing the edges of the laminate with a file is the final step in the process. This part of the job requires a little patience as you want to put a smooth, slight bevel on all the edges, without cutting into the Formica surface (see **Figure 3-4**).

Once the hardware and plumbing fixtures have been installed, and the excess glue has been cleaned off the plastic surfaces with a rag and a bit of lacquer thinner; the top is ready to be installed in the boat.

Some Additional Suggestions

If you are undertaking your first project with plastic laminate, we suggest that you buy a little extra laminate, and make up a test panel. A small square of 3/4-inch plywood would be perfectly adequate. Try each step of the laminating process on the

Figure 3-4. Dressing the Edges of Plastic Laminate

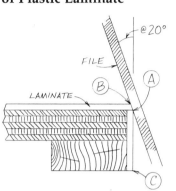

With a sharp file, and careful, deliberate strokes, file the edge of the overlapping laminate, until it is just flush with the laminate edge at point A. Then increase the angle of the file slightly and take a few additional strokes with the file to produce a clean, smooth line along the seam. Finally, take a light stroke at point B, and a few at point C to eliminate sharp edges. Keep in mind when you dress these edges, that the greater the angle of bevel at the seam, the wider the seam will appear. Therefore, it is best to try to keep the file as close to perpendicular as practical. We recommend that you do not use the beveled router bit sold for dressing a self-edge in plastic laminate. To be of any value, the bevel bit requires extremely precise adjustment which is not possible with the sloppy bearings in inexpensive routers.

test panel before proceeding to the actual workpiece. This will give you a feel for the plastic, and possibly help to avoid wasting material later. In trimming your test panel, if you find that the router bit tends to cut too deeply or to burn the edge that the pilot wheel runs on, cover that edge with a strip of masking tape before trimming.

If you do run into a problem, you can remove a piece of laminate by peeling back a corner with a putty knife, and squirting a little lacquer thinner behind the plastic. You can apply a fresh coat of contact cement and reapply the piece, or try again with a new piece.

We suggest that you cut openings for sinks and drop-in stoves and the like, before applying the laminate, and then remove the laminate in the opening with the router. Once the laminate is adhered to the substrate, it can be difficult to cut these openings without chipping the edges of the plastic. For installing hardware and fixtures, however, you can use a high-speed drill or a hole saw in the laminated surface without difficulty.

Laminating only the outside of a stiffened structure such as cabinet or countertop should present no problems, but in the case of large, unsupported panels such as shelves and cabinet doors, you should plan to laminate both sides of the panel. Formica is very effective at preventing the migration of moisture in or out of the wood substrate. As a result, laminating only one side of a large panel could later cause it to warp.

To avoid confusion, we did not mention laminating the inside edges of an opening such as the hatch to the laundry bin in our vanity. Actually, this was the first laminate we applied on this particular piece. The strips that cover the outside edges of the hatch cover are cut long, of course, and trimmed to length on the workpiece with the router. The strips that cover the inside edges of the hatch opening, on the other hand, must be cut precisely to length before they are applied. Fortunately, this is easier to do than it may sound. Simply take an accurate measurement, rough cut the strips to length with a pair of tin snips, then square up the ends of the strips to the proper length with a file. Go easy with the file, dry fitting after each few strokes, until you have a perfect fit.

A final subject which we avoided earlier, is applying plastic laminate to a curved surface. Formica will bend around a radius of 2-1/2 or 3 inches without difficulty. To bend it to a radius of 2 inches or less without cracking will require heat, relieving the back of the laminate, or both. Heat is simple to apply with a heat gun or a portable hair dryer, although laminate bent with heat will sometimes crack when it cools. If, after attempting to dry fit the laminate, you are in doubt as to whether or not it will take the required curvature, it is best to reduce its thickness by relieving the back of the plastic. Do this by clamping the plastic upside-down on the workbench, and then using a belt sander or a cabinet scraper to reduce its thickness by about half in the area of the curvature.

4

Exterior Projects and Improvements

BUILD A SUN AWNING

Even the most dedicated sun-worshipper craves shade after a bright, hot day on the water. For those of us whose goals include keeping our skin intact over time, a way to get out of the sun is imperative if we are to enjoy being in the cockpit at anchor or in a slip. The problem is that few sailboats come equipped with usable shade, at least when the sails are down. The solution to the shade problem is a sun awning.

A sun awning also solves another problem, particularly in tropical climates. By keeping the deck shaded, and by preventing the sun from streaming through deadlights and open hatches, an awning is a big help in keeping the temperature of the cabin interior at a habitable level.

An awning can take a variety of different forms depending on how sophisticated you want to make it, and how much cover you really need. Happily, most awnings can be made by anyone with even the most basic sewing skills.

The first photograph shows the most common form of awning, basically a large rectangle of cloth draped tent-like over the boom and secured by cords to the backstay and lifelines. The awning shown is aboard *Havoc*, and was made by owners Norm and Gloria Drummond in about two hours.

To get the width of the awning, you need to measure from one lifeline over the boom and down to the lifeline on the other side. It is a good idea to measure this width at the forward end of the awning, in the middle, and at the after end, so that you can

The basic boom-tent awning.

taper the awning to fit the changing beam of the boat. Otherwise, you could use a single, average width. Make a sketch, more or less to scale, with the proper dimensions shown to help you visualize the finished product.

To determine the length of the awning, measure along the boom, from wherever you want the awning to begin, all the way aft to the backstay. If they were doing it again, the Drummonds say that they would extend the awning forward almost to the mast to shade as much of the cabin top as possible.

You will also need to measure the distance from the topping lift to the backstay. When putting the awning together, you will have to make a cut along the centerline of the awning so it can straddle the topping lift (**Figure 4-1**). This cut can be joined with snaps, or with Velcro tape.

Figure out how many yards of fabric you will need, then add 10 to 15 percent more for seams. You can use almost any cloth for an awning. Many commercial awnings use a very light fabric such as ripstop nylon spinnaker cloth. This has the advantage of stowing compactly, but it has the disadvantage of being semi-

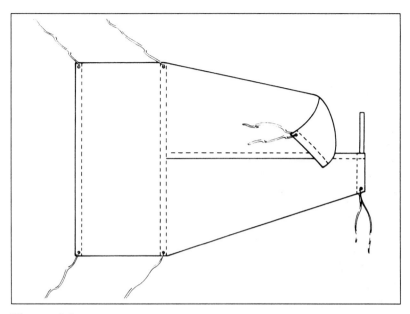

Figure 4-1.

transparent and subject to deterioration from ultraviolet light. If this is the route you want to go, ask your sailmaker if he has any flawed material he will sell you cheap. You can also buy sailcloth and other fabrics from some mail-order discount firms, notably Defender Industries (P.O. Box 820; New Rochelle, NY 10802).

We prefer a heavier, more opaque fabric, such as lightweight canvas, denim, or oxford cloth, which you can get at a local fabric shop. These natural fabrics can mildew, however. You can reduce the chances of mildew by treating the finished awning with a commercial mildew-proofer.

Acrilan is a synthetic canvas, available in several colors, and commonly used for sailcovers. At about 9.5 ounces per yard, it is much heavier than spinnaker cloth. Acrilan is also easy to sew on a home machine. It is mildew-proof and has good resistance to ultraviolet light. Even though it costs about twice as much as nylon sailcloth, acrilan is highly recommended for any type of awning or exterior canvaswork.

While almost any fabric can be used for awnings, choose a relatively soft material. Avoid Dacron sailcloth, which snaps,

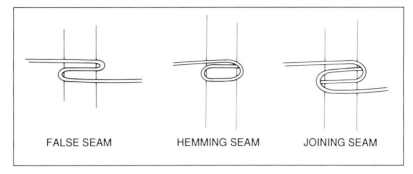

FALSE SEAM   HEMMING SEAM   JOINING SEAM

Figure 4-2.

crackles, and pops in any sort of breeze. Consider using either white or a light pastel color. Darker colors transmit less light, but they are also hotter.

For sewing the awning, there are three basic seams you need to know: the hemming seam, the joining seam, and the false seam (**Figure 4-2**). The false seam is used in wide fabrics to keep the material from stretching. False seams were widely used when sails were made of cotton, but are rarely needed with today's stable synthetic sailcloth. With a soft material, use a false seam in the middle of each full-width panel.

Take care to make the seam widths even. A seam width of about 3/4 inch looks good. If grommets are used in the seams, the seams will have to be slightly wider. Be sure to check the size of the grommets before making the seams.

An alternative to grommets is a simple loop of light line (1/4 inch or 3/8 inch) whipped at the ends and hand-sewn to the cloth with waxed nylon sail twine. It is a good solution if you do not have a tool for setting grommets. Be sure to sew through the line as well as around it when attaching the loop.

When you are ready to cut and sew your awning together, install the Velcro or other closure at the cut for the topping lift, and attach the grommets or loops at the appropriate places. Along the side of the awning, every three feet should be about right. That's it for the basic boom-tent awning, but there are other variations you might think about.

The major problem with the tent awning is that headroom is limited, except in the very middle. For this reason, awnings with

A low, curved awning will keep rain from entering the companionway and help to keep the cabin cool.

spreaders, allowing additional headroom out to the edge of the awning, are popular. The battens slide into pockets to stretch the awning across the boat. The ends of the battens are tied under slight tension to the lifelines or toerails. By adjusting the length of these lines, the awning can be tilted to one side or the other to suit the angle of the sun. As with the simpler design, a longitudinal slit, closed with Velcro, may be necessary to clear the topping lift.

Battens can be made from wood, aluminum tubing, or bamboo, with bamboo perhaps the most satisfactory. Bamboo is light, tough, springy, and can stand a lot of abuse. Because it checks and splits badly, tape it at about 6-inch intervals between the nodes. For awning battens on anything but a really big boat, bamboo of 3/4 inch to one inch in diameter will do the trick.

The only complication in making a battened awning is that the batten pockets must be designed in. Pockets 2 to 3 inches wide, with about 3 to 4 feet between battens, should be about right for most boats. Ties of lightweight cord can be sewn into the ends of the pockets to retain the battens.

Another type of awning is the low, curved awning. It consists of nothing more than a tapered length of cloth running from the mast to a foot or so aft of the companionway. It is given shape by two curved lengths of aluminum rod which fit into pockets at

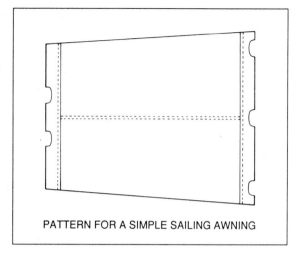

PATTERN FOR A SIMPLE SAILING AWNING

Figure 4-3.

either end of the awning. The awning is hung from the boom and tied down to the grab rails on top of the cabin. This creates an air space above the cabin top. Though this air space is only a few inches high, it helps greatly in keeping the cabin cool. Any awning which covers the cabin will achieve the same effect. The advantages of this particular type of awning are that it is unobtrusive, has little windage, and does not hinder movement on deck. As a result, you may be able to use it more often than other types of awnings which tend get in the way when underway or to get out of hand when the wind pipes up.

In common with most other types of awnings, the low, curved awning allows the companionway slide to be left open under conditions of heavy dew, mist, or light rain. The design and construction are simple. The only complications are deciding on the curvature of the supporting rods, and adjusting the width to accommodate the fact that most cabins narrow as they run forward. In the awning shown, the forward rod is only 4 inches above the top of the cabin.

So far we have talked about awnings which can only be used when a boat is stationary or under power. But what about a sailing awning? Of course it is possible to sail with a Bimini top over the cockpit, but Bimini tops are expensive, provide relatively little shade, and no matter how they are installed, the frame is always in the way.

The sailing awning, an inexpensive alternative to the Bimini top, is shown here rigged over the cockpit.

A simpler idea is a slightly tapered, battened awning tied to the backstay bridle aft, and held forward by lines running to lifeline stanchions on either side. If you do not have a split backstay, you can lash the awning to the single backstay and tie the ends down to the stern rail. The forward end is held up by a line permanently fixed about ten feet up the backstay. This line has a halyard clip at its lower end, and when not in use, clips out of the way on the backstay.

This awning is about as unobtrusive as an awning can be, and can be rigged in a minute or two. When approaching a harbor or encountering a situation in which the crew must have maximum maneuverability, letting go the forward lines (but not the upper lines) causes the whole thing to drift back out of the way against the backstay.

The awning should be narrow enough so that the crew can still sit on the cockpit coamings when the awning is rigged. If that is not important to you, a wider awning would give more shade. Even in its narrow form, however, the awning can be cocked toward the sun by readjusting the lengths of the forward lines.

To avoid grommets and loops, the awning can be designed with scallops cut out of the batten pockets. These cutouts allow the lines to be tied directly to the bamboo battens so that the lines can serve both to keep the battens in their pockets and to hold the awning in place (**Figure 4-3**). The cutouts are hemmed or finished with binding tape. A false seam is used down the middle to reduce stretch.

This awning can be finished in an hour or two for a cost of less than ten or fifteen dollars. It could be made with any lightweight fabric, although a mildew-proof synthetic fabric would be best.

The varieties of awnings are almost endless, and only you can decide which works best for your boat, and your type of sailing. On a hot sunny day, a little shade will easily be worth the effort expended.

THE PRACTICAL SAILBAG

For setting and dousing a headsail, we concede that roller furling is easier and luff grooves are faster. Still, hanks on the headsail strike us as a more seamanlike way to attach a sail to a stay and to facilitate changing headsails underway. The most troublesome aspect of the hanked-on headsail is the problem of getting the sail into the sailbag while it is still hanked on, and then getting the bulky sailbag in and out of the cockpit locker or companionway. If you like the convenience of leaving the headsail hanked on overnight when cruising, you should consider building the Practical Sailbag.

The Practical Sailbag is a variation on the sausage bag in that the sail is flaked on top of it, and then the bag is wrapped around the sail and zipped up. The sail remains hanked to the headstay while it is being bagged. Once the bag is secured, it can be used to store the sail either detached from the stay, or with the sail still hanked on.

Like a sausage bag, the bag is laid open on the deck under the sail. After the jib is lowered, the clew is pulled aft and the sail is loosely flaked. The clew is placed at the after end of the bag with the sheets either attached or removed, and the drawstring at the after end is pulled tight and tied. Then the two sides of the bag are pulled up around the sail and zipped closed. If the sail is left hanked on, the forward flap or zipper closes over the stay and the hanks. If the sail is being removed from the headstay, the hanks are then unhooked and the forward end closed to form a bag. Finally, the ties around the bag are pulled tight and tied.

The result is a bagged sail fully 30 percent smaller than the

The Practical Sailbag works equally well as a conventional sailbag with the jib detached from the headstay, or as a sailcover with the sail hanked on.

same sail stuffed into a conventional sailbag. The time and effort to bag the sail and remove it from the stay is about the same; the time to bag it and leave it attached is considerably less. Best of all, the bag drops unimpeded into a seat locker and lifts out with nary a struggle.

The Practical Sailbag represents no technological break-through; other sailors and sailmakers have come up with comparable bags. Nevertheless, it does work, and its cost is modest—

Figure 4-4.

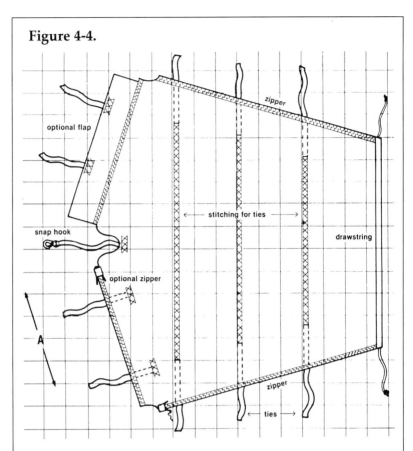

Scale drawing of the Practical Sailbag over a grid can be used to figure dimensions for any size jib. For bagging a jib left hanked to the headstay, the critical dimension is "A" which must be long enough to reach from under the jib tack fitting to the top of the uppermost hank. If this dimension cannot actually be measured on the boat, figure 2-1/2 inches per hank with a rope luff.

Do not stitch the ties all the way from one side to the other; the unstitched portion allows them to compress the bag when they are tied tightly. The flap on the forward edge is an alternative to a zipper. Either can be used although we prefer the zipper, even if it is a bit more costly. Zippers should zip from forward aft and from tack to head. The snap hook on the strap allows the open bag to be secured to the headstay before the jib is lowered.

For a 250 square foot jib, the major dimensions are approximately: 54 inches on the centerline; 60 inches across the widest point; 32 inches up the forestay (Dimension A); 36 inches across the open after end.

about $60 to $90 if made by a sailmaker, perhaps $25 if you make it yourself.

The cloth for the bag can be either nylon sailbag cloth or acrylic sailcover cloth. Acrylic is harder sew, but offers better sunlight protection, and would be the better choice if the bag will be used primarily as a cover with the sail left hanked to its stay. In this case, the bag can be color coordinated to match the awning or mainsail cover.

In cutting out the bag, plan to make it a bit oversized. Resewing it a bit smaller is simple if it proves necessary, or it can be left spacious and the ties used to take up the excess.

INSTALL A COCKPIT SHOWER

What a luxury it is to be able to have a fresh water shower after a salty swim or as a refresher during the endless dog days of August. If your boat already has a pressure water system, a cockpit shower can be installed for less than $100 and with only a few hours of labor.

The first step is to determine the location of the spigots and the hand-held showerhead. Locating the hardware in the shallow cockpit seat locker is often easiest and keeps all the components out of the elements. A primary consideration is adequate clearance behind the mounting area for the spigot assembly.

The spigot assembly can be purchased from a local plumbing supplier. Choose a low-profile model for a conventional stall shower which needs only about 1-1/2 inches of mounting clearance behind it. A standard hand-held shower with hose is screwed directly into the outlet base of the spigot assembly. Various lengths of chrome-plated nipples are available to fit between the spigot and shower if necessary. The cost for the entire assembly should be about $50.

If your boat has both hot and cold water, you will want to plumb the cockpit shower into both existing lines. With a cold-water system only, you will use only one side of the shower spigot, but the hot-water tap will be available if you add a water heater at a later date.

Flexible polybutyl (PB) tubing and plastic fittings make the plumbing job simple. The tubing itself is less than half the cost of

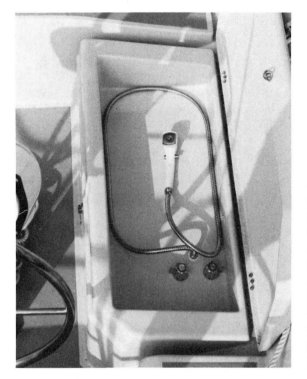

A shallow cockpit locker is the perfect place to install a cockpit shower. By installing a partition in the locker to protect the shower controls, it is still possible to use part of the locker for storage.

copper and about two-thirds cheaper than reinforced vinyl hose. The tubing is suitable for hot water, can freeze without breaking, and is chemically inert so it leaves no taste. With the large assortment of adapters available, you can use PB tubing on virtually any type of existing plumbing system. You don't have to be a professional plumber to make leak-free joints either, thanks to the simplicity of the fittings. If your local plumbing supplier does not carry polybutyl plumbing parts, try a large recreational vehicle dealer.

The actual plumbing itself is straightforward; simply cut both the hot and cold water lines at a convenient spot and install the plastic T-fittings. The only tools necessary to install this type of plumbing are an adjustable wrench and a sharp utility knife or razor blade.

For a relatively small investment and a few hours of effort, you can install a cockpit shower, enhancing both your enjoyment and the value of your boat.

DO-IT-YOURSELF FENDER BOARDS

Fender boards are almost a necessity when docking against pilings. They are designed to ride outboard of two fenders, protecting a larger section of the topsides than the two fenders could provide alone. Without fender boards, no matter how you position and secure your boat and fenders, the movement of the tide and the boat will invariably displace the fenders relative to the pilings. The result? Dinged and scratched topsides.

The simplest form of fender board is adequate for most docking needs. All that is required is a three- or four-foot length of 2x4, 2x6, or 2x8. As a guide, we would use a 2x4 for a 20-footer, a 2x6 for a 30-footer, and a 2x8 for a 40-footer. On a larger boat, you may want to use a slightly longer board—perhaps as long as six feet. A board longer than six feet, however, will probably take two people to handle and be a nuisance to store.

For the simplest type of fender board, you can purchase standard framing lumber, which may be one of several species of spruce, pine, or hemlock. Make sure that it does not have any large knots in the middle of the board which could cause it to break under heavy loading. A hardwood like oak or ash will take more abuse, but the extra weight can make the fender board difficult for one person to handle.

Drill a hole slightly larger than the diameter of the suspension or drop lines (a 9/16-inch hole for 1/2-inch line, for example) through the larger dimension at either end of the board, about six inches from either end. Then round the ends of the plank and chamfer or round all the edges.

The drop lines should be long enough to suspend the plank down to the waterline from whatever stanchions or cleats you plan to use. After threading the lines through the holes, tie a figure-8 stopper knot at the bottom of each line, and the boards are ready to use.

Because of the abuse fender boards are intended to take, painting or varnishing them may be a waste of time. And, because you want a fender board to be as gentle as possible to your boat, complications like metal hanging straps or eye bolts are best avoided.

You can use your fender board with conventional round

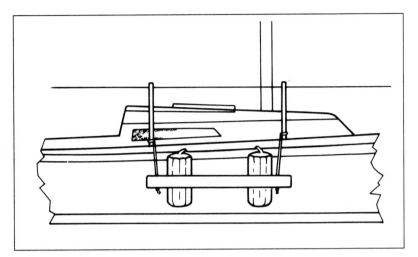

Above: Made from two fenders and a short length of framing lumber, the simplest type of fender board is adequate for most docking needs. Below: A laminated fender board with 1/8-inch spacers at each end.

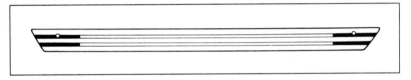

fenders, or you can purchase solid rubber cushions made specifically for attaching to 2x4 or 2x6 boards. The rubber cushions do not give the board quite as much standoff from the hull that a large round fender will, but because they are permanently attached to the fender board, there is no risk that they will pop out of position, allowing the board to rub against the topsides.

The one embellishment you might wish to consider, if you have the time and inclination, is a laminated fender board. This board is composed of three layers of fir, hickory, or ash with the layers separated by 1/8-inch strips of wood. The spacer strips are epoxied in at either end with the object of creating a leaf-spring effect.

Although we don't imagine that a laminated fender board is much more effective than a length of solid 2x6, they certainly look more impressive than a piece of framing lumber. Only you can decide which sort of board would satisfy you.

LAID TEAK DECKS

There was a time when laid decks—teak, yellow pine, or fir—were the hallmark of a true yacht. The bare wood gave secure footing, was easy to maintain, and provided reasonable protection from leaks. Since the advent of fiberglass, those same laid decks, almost universally of teak, have continued to represent that hallmark. They have become more a functional, cosmetic feature, however, rather than a structural one.

Almost no project can do more to dress up a boat than some laid decking, and it is a job the average boatowner can do himself. Decks, cockpit seats, cockpit sole, hatch covers, and the cabin sole all lend themselves to being planked (or sheathed) with teak decking.

Let's start by examining what such a project entails. Laid teak decking is expensive. As a purchased option on a production 35-footer, it may run as much as $6000 to $8000. The present cost of teak bought in small lots runs to nearly $10 per board foot, and the price of glues and caulking approaches that of vintage cognac. A reasonable estimate for materials alone is about $8 per square foot, to say nothing of the labor, whether you pay a professional or do it yourself putting a fair value on your time and skills.

The idea is to lay a deck that looks traditional and solid. However, since the underlying structure, usually plywood or cored fiberglass, is strong enough not to need the planking, the planking can be reasonably thin. The teak can be as thin as 1/8 to 3/16 inch thick, up to about 3/8 inch at the most. At this thickness, the weight of the decking is not so much that it should seriously decrease stability.

The problem with laying deck this thin is that fastening is a problem. If it were screwed to the underlying deck, the bungs (plugs) used over the fastening would be so thin they would be difficult to keep in place and could be quickly worn through.

One solution is to glue the decking down and avoid the use of any permanent fasteners. With modern epoxies, this system has been used for years by production boatbuilders, and lends itself to amateur use. The secret is to use the right glue and only as many temporary fasteners as necessary to hold the planking

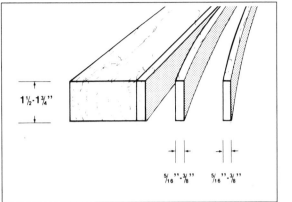

Figure 4-4.

in place while the glue sets. When the fasteners are removed, the holes they were in are counterbored and bungs set in. Only you know that what looks like traditionally fastened decking is just as strong but was easier to lay than the "real thing."

Tools and Materials

To lay decking in this fashion, start by measuring the area you wish to plank. It is best to work with smaller areas such as the cockpit sole or hatches before tackling the deck itself; laying a whole deck is a monumental project.

To determine the area, draw it to scale and decide what

Figure 4-5.

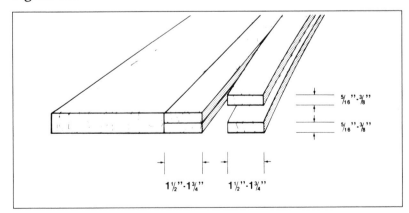

pattern of planking is best suited to it. Avoid trying to bend the planking to follow a curve; the thin wood we are using is hard to bend without splitting. Round all dimensions upward to take waste into account and buy plenty of wood for all the decking you plan to do.

The items you will need include the following:

WOOD. Teak is best bought dressed: sawn and planed (on one side, the top) to finished dimensions. The planks should be 1-1/2 inches to 1-3/4 inches wide for the most "authentic" look. There are two ways to have it sawn: rip a teak plank of the proper thickness to produce slices of the width of your planking (**Figure 4-4**); or resaw thinner boards that have been ripped into strips the width of the planking (**Figure 4-5**). The latter may be a bit more expensive, but it may also be easier to obtain dressed 1-inch boards than the 2-inch dressed boards needed for the former.

GLUE. For best adhesion use a quality epoxy for laminating wood, thickened so that it stays in place when spread in a generous film. Start with regular laminating epoxy resin and add chopped strands or fibers (not microspheres, microballoons or other mere thickening agents that do not serve to retain the strength of the glue). The glue should have the viscosity of mayonnaise (a lump should hang from an inverted putty knife without dripping off).

CAULKING. The planking we are putting on uses caulking only cosmetically, not for permanent waterproofing. Our suggestion is black Life-Caulk (a one-part polysulfide made by BoatLife, Inc.) in 10-ounce cartridges.

FASTENERS. Since the fasteners are temporary, we suggest #10 steel pan-head sheetmetal screws 1/2 inch long. Flat-head screws tend to split thin teak if driven in too hard near the ends of planks.

3/8-INCH TEAK BUNGS. It is better to cut your own bungs from the same stock you are using. Ready-made bungs may not match the color and texture of the teak you are using.

SPACERS. You will also need a small quantity of scrap wood the thickness of the seams between the planks (such as strips of 1/4-inch plywood a few inches long). These serve as spacers so that the seams are a uniform width.

TOOLS. For laying this type of decking, the tools required are found in most home workshops:
- **Power hand drill**
- **Power sander**, orbital ("vibrating" type), plus sandpaper
- **3/8-inch counterbore bit** and matching bung cutter
- **Square**, either a framing square or a tri-square
- **Screwdriver**
- **Putty knife** for spreading glue
- **Cartridge type caulking gun**
- **Miter box and saw**
- **Table saw** with carbide blade
- **Weights** such as five-pound lead pigs or bricks

Laying the Decking

Start by thoroughly sanding the surfaces on which the planking is to be laid, and then wipe down the area with acetone. Unless all traces of wax are removed, it may prevent adhesion of the glue. If in doubt, mix a small drop of glue, let it harden in a droplet on the gelcoat, and then try to tap it loose. If the epoxy is adhering properly, it should take a chip of gelcoat with it.

From the plan or pattern made to determine the amount of materials, cut all the pieces of planking to fit. If the area has deck fittings or follows a curved contour, use a precise pattern and first fit the planking to these shapes, dry fitting the pieces with screws but without epoxy. Then lay out the straight pieces of planking to check the dimensions. Once you start gluing and screwing you won't want to be interrupted by the need for cutting or fine fitting. If you have a choice, start at a straight edge and work toward a curve or a taper.

When the planking has been cut and fitted, mix and thicken the glue, enough to do about one hour's work (less if the temperature is hot or the deck is being laid in the sun). Remember to mix the two-part glue first, then add the fibers.

By using a thick glue, there should be no need to predrill pilot

All of the pieces for this section of decking have been cut and rough fitted using a 1/4-inch space between pieces. The pattern selected for this decking uses a frame of the same width as the planking with mitered corners.

holes for the screws before setting each piece of planking in place. The stickiness of the glue, plus the use of spacers, should let you drill while holding the plank without its slipping. Put a wood stop or piece of tape on the drill so that the holes will only be as deep as the screws are long. Remember, you only need to use enough screws so that the plank stays firmly in place while the glue cures. On smooth, flat surfaces, weights alone will probably suffice.

Spread the glue thickly, especially in localized hollows. The virtue of epoxy is that, unlike many other adhesives, it will bridge gaps; that is, epoxy retains its strength even where the two surfaces being glued are not in direct contact. Use that virtue in laying the decking—but don't allow voids.

Lay each plank in the glue and move it around enough to assure that the glue transfers to the entire underside of the wood. It is okay if the adhesive squeezes up a bit between the planks as you set them in place, but don't let so much get pushed up that it fills the seam.

As soon as one plank is in place and screwed or weighted

Taping the edges of the seams, and smoothing the seam compound with a putty knife, will eliminate the need for heavy sanding of the finished surface.

down, spread more glue and go on to the next. If using planking with square edges, set spacers between the planks at regular intervals (every 2 feet or so) and push the next plank tight against the spacer before drilling and fastening. As long lengths of teak may be slightly warped, you may need a screw or two in mid-span to keep the edge against the spacers.

As soon as the glue has begun to set, gently slide the spacers out; if left in place, the glue at the bottom of the seams will make them stick as fast as the planking. Removing them later could result in chipping the edges of the planking.

Once the adhesive under the straight planks has cured, remove any edge pieces that were temporarily screwed down, spread glue under them and fasten them down. Carefully clean up any glue that pushes out on the outside edges of planks with acetone on a clean rag. Even a thin film of epoxy will show up as yellow and unsightly when it cures, and will be almost impossible to remove.

Finally, after all the pieces are in place and the glue has cured completely; remove all the screws, redrill with the counterbore almost to the bottom of each plank, and plug with bungs. Glue the bungs in (this is one time it pays to glue bungs, as there will never be any reason to remove them).

The finished decking, ready for a coat of sealer.

Finishing Up

When all of the planking has been bunged and the glue is dry, carefully chisel the bungs off almost flush. Sand the new decking well with moderately coarse sandpaper (80 grit). If any plank stands higher than the surrounding ones, sand or plane it level.

Next, tape along each seam edge with masking tape and fill the seams with black caulking compound, overfilling the seams slightly. Then drag a putty knife blade along the top of each seam to smooth and level the compound. Remove the tape and allow the caulking to cure.

If during finishing, you discover that any planking has a void under it (it may be springy or a tap with a hard object will make a hollow sound), drill a 3/8-inch hole through the teak into the void. Use that hole to fill the void with glue using a glue syringe, then bung the hole.

Sand the whole area with progressively finer sandpaper grits until the surface is smooth, rounding any sharp corners slightly. Finally, apply a teak dressing or sealer after you are certain the caulking is completely cured.

A BETTER WAY TO MOUNT DECK HARDWARE

Improperly mounted deck hardware, stanchion bases, and pulpit bases are not only the cause of troublesome cosmetic problems aboard a fiberglass boat, but could be the source of a disaster for both ship and crew on a boat built in any material.

The dangers of a cleat, turning block, or stanchion base pulling through the deck are obvious. Not always so obvious (at least at first), is the problem of gelcoat cracks radiating from the attached hardware. These cracks are usually the result of un-equally stressed fasteners, or inadequate distribution of hardware loads. Frequently, a boat is received from the builder with local cracks already developed. Once the deck gets dirty enough, these minute cracks start to show up as tiny spider webs in the surrounding gelcoat. While repairing these cracks is a fairly difficult cosmetic fix, the underlying problem—poor mounting—is usually easy to correct in most cases.

A common problem with stanchion mounting is caused when the base straddles the inward-turning flange of the hull-to-deck joint. Frequently, the outboard bolts will go through both the hull and deck, while the inboard fasteners merely go through

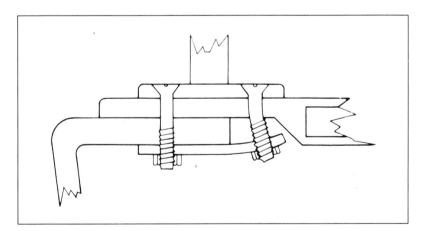

Shock loading on deck hardware can distort backing plates and crack the gelcoat or even fracture the laminate.

the deck. When a backing plate straddles the edge of the hull flange under the deck, it is frequently distorted as the bolts fastening the stanchion bases are tightened. Tightening the bolts when the backing plate does not lie flush to the underside of the deck inevitably causes local stresses in the deck, frequently resulting in the characteristic spider web of gelcoat cracks.

To avoid the problem, some builders simply use oversize washers under the nuts of through-deck bolts. These are not adequate to resist strong local loads, such as leaning hard against a lifeline stanchion. The proper solution is a backing plate of a rigid material, at least the size of the base of the fitting.

It is fairly common for builders to use fiberglass backing plates, cut from discarded sections of moldings such as cutouts for hatches and ports. While a fiberglass backing plate is better than nothing, it can easily split or distort when bolts are tightened, reducing its effectiveness.

With stainless steel or aluminum hardware, fastened with stainless steel bolts, the best material to use for backing plates is aluminum, between 1/8 and 1/4 inch thick. Aluminum can be worked with ordinary woodworking tools. It can be easily cut with a sabre saw, and sharp corners can be rounded quickly with a file or aluminum oxide sandpaper. Aluminum is also extremely light in weight. You can usually buy scrap aluminum

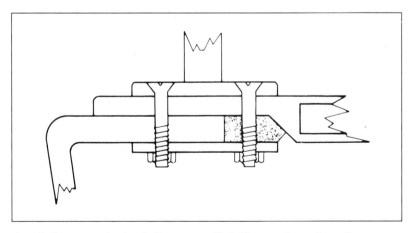

A pad of epoxy and microballoons or milled fibers under awkwardly mounted deck hardware can prevent uneven loads on the deck.

Aluminum backing plates are easily cut from scrap sheetmetal with a jig saw or band saw.

from a scrap-metal dealer. Although the price will vary, you should be able to buy a lifetime supply of backing-plate material for ten dollars or less.

If you are making your own backing plates using a sabre saw, invest in a good supply of metal cutting blade—about 12 teeth per inch will produce clean cuts in aluminum up to 3/8 inch thick. Don't try to use old blades, or blades designed for other uses. You will be amazed at the difference a sharp blade of the right type makes.

When drilling holes in backing plates, be sure to drill slightly oversize to allow for bolts that are not perfectly perpendicular to the plate. To drill for a 1/4-inch bolt, use a 9/32-inch drill for the backing plate holes. The easiest way to insure proper alignment for the holes is to clamp the backing plate to the base of the fitting before drilling pilot holes, using the hardware fastening holes as a template. Don't drill these pilot holes oversize, as you would enlarge the fastening holes in the hardware, making them more likely to leak.

Alternatively, if you have a helper, you can drill the pilot holes by simply holding the backing plate under the deck and removing the bolts from the already-attached hardware, one at a time. In the case of stanchions, this method may prove to be more effort than simply removing the stanchion base, but it may be less work than removing a bow pulpit or stern rail.

Whether you are installing new backing plates, or simply correcting an improper installation, the method is the same.

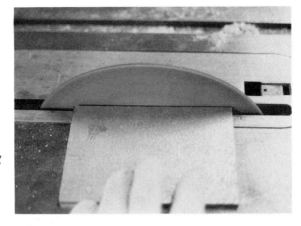

A disk sander or sanding disk mounted in a table saw is helpful for cleaning up the edges and rounding the corners on an aluminum backing plate.

Unless the underside of the deck in the way of the backing plate is smooth and flat, you can take advantage of that miracle mixture—epoxy and microballoons. If there is any such thing as a panacea for the modern boatowner, it is epoxy resin filled with microballoons or chopped fibers. The epoxy and filler mixture is used to create a firm pad under the backing plate, straddling and smoothing out any irregularities in the underside of the deck surface, even irregularities as pronounced as the inside lap of the hull-to-deck joint.

First, make sure that the hardware fastening bolts line up with the holes in the backing plate. Next, thoroughly wax the surface of the backing plate that will lie against the underside of the deck; also wax the hardware bolts. Waxing allows you to remove the bolts and backing plate in the future. If you do not wax them, your installation will be permanent, and few things on a boat should be that permanent.

Make a dry run to be sure that you have not overlooked anything. Then, mix only enough resin and microballoons to do one piece of hardware. The epoxy mixture must be fairly dry to keep it from running out of the gap between the backing plate and the underside of the deck. You will have about the right consistency when the mixture can be troweled onto the backing plate without sagging off.

Trowel the mixture onto the backing plate at least as thick as the largest irregularity to be bridged. Any excess will be squeezed out when the nuts are tightened. Be sure that you put

The finished back-ing plate should be at least as large as the piece of hard-ware it backs up.

bedding compound under the heads of the bolts, and under the base of the fitting if it has been removed. With the plate, bolts, and nuts in place, evenly tighten the nuts using a socket wrench, with a helper above decks holding the head of the bolt or machine screw tight with a wrench or screwdriver. Do not tighten by turning the bolts from above; you will turn the bedding compound out from under the heads of the bolts. Tighten the bolts only enough to bring the plate evenly in position. When bridging the inside of the hull-to-deck joint, you may end up with an epoxy pad that is 1/2 inch thick at one end, and only thick enough to fill slight irregularities at the other.

You can now use a putty knife to clean up the epoxy that squeezed out when the plate pulled up to the deck. You can make a handful of neat, disposable "putty knives" by cutting a bundle of wooden tongue depressors in half, using the round end to produce a radiused corner, and the square end to clean up the excess epoxy on flat surfaces and in square corners. Most epoxy is water soluble before it kicks, so warm water and a sponge can be used around the edges for a perfectly neat clean up.

If the epoxy is too thin, and wants to sag out of the gap between the plate and the deck, use masking tape to hold it in place. Pull the tape off as soon as the epoxy kicks off, and clean up any runs or dribbles with sandpaper.

When the epoxy has cured, the nuts can be tightened a little more. Lock washers used under the nuts will keep the nuts from backing off without the need to tighten the fasteners excessively.

If the fasteners protrude more than 1/4 inch or so below the nuts, you may want to cut them off flush with a hacksaw. Do not use end nippers for this, as many boatbuilders do, because you may break the seal between the fastener and the bedding compound while working the nippers back and forth to break off the end of the bolt.

*   *   *

This method can be used almost anywhere above and below decks to fill in major surface irregularities. When used above decks, the hardware and fasteners must be removed and bedded after the epoxy has cured, and the exposed edges of the epoxy "pad" painted or gel-coated to match the surrounding area.

When weather conditions and lurching crewmembers combine to put extra stresses on lifelines and deck hardware, it is truly comforting to know that the hardware is mounted in as effective a manner as possible; and the prevention of crazed and scarred deck gelcoat is a bonus well worth the extra effort.

FAIRING THROUGH-HULL FITTINGS FOR LIGHT-AIR PERFORMANCE

How is the light-air performance of your boat? As good as you would like it to be, or could it use some improvement? You can measurably improve the light-air performance of most boats with little more than a bit of elbow grease. The secret is to pay attention to underwater fairness and smoothness.

In light air, a major portion of the total resistance of a sailboat hull results from skin friction. The smoother the boat's bottom,

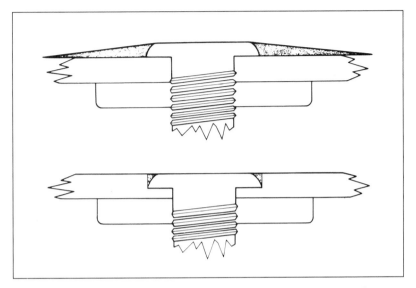

Fairing in a through-hull fitting (top illustration) is usually easier than recessing, but it is somewhat less effective for reducing drag. If the hull is thick enough, a surface-mount fitting (bottom) can be recessed flush.

the less power is required to drive it to a given speed. Put another way, given two boats identical in every way, the boat with the smoother bottom will be faster in light air. The difference will not be much, but it will be measurable. Around the race course or at the end of a day of sailing, the difference could add up to several minutes or several miles.

"Smooth" and "rough" are, of course, relative terms. For practical purposes, the bottom of a displacement-type sailboat can be considered smooth if the surface varies no more than 2 mils (two thousandths of an inch)! Before you throw up your hands is despair, it should be pointed out that a surface of this quality is not that hard to achieve. The surface of most fiberglass boats is this smooth when it comes from the mold. The smoothness begins to be compromised, however, as soon as through-hull fittings, transducers, and bottom paint are added.

You can begin your quest for a fast bottom by recessing or fairing in the through-hull fittings that protrude beyond the surface of the hull, particularly in the forward half of the boat. Typically, this means the head intake and discharge fittings.

Whether you decide to recess fittings or fair them in depends on the hull construction, and the amount of time and money you are willing to spend.

Fairing In Through-Hulls

The standard surface-mounted through-hull, with rounded edges on an external flange, is more suited to fairing in than to recessing. Through-hull fittings specifically designed to be recessed have either a flange with square sides or a flange which is beveled on the underside. If you want to spend the least amount of money and time, you can simply fair in surface-mounted through-hulls; if you want the least resistance, you will have to recess or replace them.

If you have a small boat with a fairly thin skin, it will probably be safer to fair in the through-hulls rather than to recess them, which requires the removal of some of the hull laminate. Likewise, if the hull is cored, and the outer laminate is thin, it is safer to fair in than to recess, unless the laminate is solid in the way of the through-hull fittings. It is safe to say that if the hull is less than 3/8 inch thick at the location of the through-hull, you should probably fair it in rather than attempt to recess the fitting.

Fairing in a fitting is pretty much the same, regardless of the hull material. With metal boats, however, you must be careful not damage the barrier coat between the metal and bottom paint. If you expose the steel or aluminum, you must build up the barrier system again before fairing in. The adhesion of the fairing putty is, of course, limited to the strength of the barrier coat's adhesion to the base metal, but this is not usually a problem with modern epoxy primers and fairing compounds.

Somewhat less care is required with a wood or fiberglass hull. Bottom paint surrounding the through-hull to be faired in should be removed, and the gelcoat or wood sanded with medium-grit paper to prepare the surface for the application of the fairing compound.

The larger the area over which you fair in the fitting, the more effective the job will be in terms of reducing drag. Obviously, at some point, fairing in over an increasingly large area simply does not pay off. As a general rule, it is sufficient to fair a through-hull over a circular area with a radius equal to about 4 inches for every 1/8 inch that the fitting protrudes beyond the hull surface.

The actual fairing process is straightforward. Remember to remove the bottom paint and to give the surface some "tooth" by sanding in the area to be faired. In addition, the surface of the through-hull fitting should also be sanded to increase the adhesion of the fairing compound.

Start by drawing a circle on the hull around the fitting to define the area to be faired in. This area, and the outside of the through-hull fitting, should receive a prime coat of clear epoxy resin to improve the bonding of the fairing compound.

Epoxy-based fairing compounds are preferable to polyester-based compounds. You can make your own using epoxy resin, milled fibers, and either microballoons or microspheres, or you can use a premixed putty. Making your own putty allows you to control the viscosity, making a putty as wet or dry as you need.

Using a wide putty knife or a flexible spreader of the type used in autobody work, trowel the putty onto the unfilled prime coat of resin. Smooth the mixture on the hull, tapering the thickness from the edge of the through-hull out to the circle you have drawn on the hull. Get the fairing compound as smooth a you can, tapering as evenly as possible. The smoother you put it on in the initial application, the less sanding and spot filling will be needed after the first coat has cured.

Once the fairing compound has set up, fair it in to the surrounding hull with sandpaper, making the transition as smooth as possible. Trowel on another coat of putty in any low spots, if necessary. Low spots can be detected by running a straightedge over the faired area; in any area where daylight shows under the straightedge, fill with more compound.

Once you are satisfied with the smoothness of the job, prime the area with a two-part epoxy primer, extending the primer out to cover any adjacent gelcoat that has been sanded. Finally, wet sand the entire area smooth before applying bottom paint.

Recessing Through-Hulls

Although fairing in through-hulls is quick and inexpensive, recessing the fitting flush with the surface is somewhat more effective for reducing drag. Recessing is usually more work,

Three types of through-hull fittings. From left to right: a conventional sur-face-mount fitting, a typical American-style flush fitting, and a European-style flush fitting.

however, and may cost more if you do not already have the tools to do the job.

Special through-hull fittings are made for recessed mounting. Oddly enough, the ones we have seen are really a poor design for the job, because they are fairly difficult to install, and have a flange that is too thick to use in the typical fiberglass boat without reinforcement on the inside of the hull. The flush fittings work best if the hull skin is 5/8 inch thick or more, which means that they are probably designed either for wooden boats or large fiberglass boats.

Recessed or flush fittings are frequently used in fiberglass boats with cored hulls, since the total hull thickness is usually enough to accept them without excessive weakening of the layup. However, the core material must be removed around the through-hull, and solid fiberglass laid up in its place. This is far easier to do during the original hull layup than after the hull has been completed.

Cutting the mortise for a recessed through-hull is the hardest job. Start with a hole saw of the same diameter as the flange of the through-hull fitting, cutting through the outer hull skin, concentric with the existing hole for the through-hull. One problem you will encounter in recessing an existing fitting is that there will be no solid laminate to hold the pilot bit for the hole saw. The simplest way around this is to carve a wood plug to fill the existing hole, then drill a small hole in the center of the plug for the pilot bit. Slight errors in concentricity can be eliminated later by grinding or sanding.

Once the hole has been cut through the outer skin, dig out the core material with a sharp knife or chisel around the hole for a distance of an inch or more. Clean the remains of the core material thoroughly from the inner surfaces of both fiberglass skins. What you are going to end up with is a solid glass section of hull in the way of the through-hull fitting, and you want to remove all traces of core material that might inhibit the bond between the hull skins and the new glass you put in.

Test the fit of the through-hull fitting in the holes you have cut in the hull. The fitting must be held in place while the new glass layup cures, with as little movement as possible. A retaining nut, designed to hold the fitting in place when it is installed without a seacock, will probably be adequate for securing the fitting while the new fiberglass cures.

To fill the cavity created by removing core material, you will need loose fiberglass fibers, or chopped strand mat, which easily pulls apart. Also required are rubber gloves, acetone, and polyester resin. To keep the resin from sticking to the through-hull fitting, thoroughly wax the fitting, filling the threads as much as possible. Also wax the retaining nut that will be used to hold the fitting in place. The idea is to pack the area where you have removed the core material with a thick mixture of fibers and resin, and then insert the through-hull in place. When the glass mixture cures, you should have a perfect imprint of the fitting in the hull, with solid fiberglass surrounding the fitting. The hull will be locally reinforced, and there will be no possibility of water penetrating the core.

Because polyester resin cures quickly, you will have to work fast once it is catalyzed; use the minimum amount of catalyst in your resin. Make the fiberglass mixture dense, using more glass than resin. Brush the inside surfaces of the hull skins with unfilled resin to seal the edges of the core before jamming the mix in. And finally, clean up any drops of resin on the outside of the hull with acetone before the resin kicks off, or mask off the area of the hull with polyethylene. Because you have to work quickly with the catalyzed fiberglass mixture, it would be helpful to have another person assisting at this stage. The helper will be most useful on the inside of the boat, installing the retaining nut and holding the through-hull in position.

To insure that the fitting will be perfectly flush in the final installation, the through-hull should actually be recessed slightly below the outer surface of the skin during the molding process. This allows a little extra room for bedding compound under the flange when the fitting is actually installed.

As soon as the resin mixture has kicked off, remove the through-hull. Chances are that it will be lightly bonded in place, no matter how thoroughly you wax it. Light tapping with a wood or plastic mallet, or a hammer and a soft-wood block, should free it from the hull.

Before final installation of the through-hull, heat it with a propane torch to remove the wax. Remember that paraffin is flammable, so hold the fitting with pliers or set it on the ground before heating.

Recessing in Solid Hulls

Installing flush fittings in a wood hull is easier than in a fiberglass hull, since the planking is thick, there is no core to remove, and a backing block should already be in place under the seacock. Most solid fiberglass hulls, however, simply are not thick enough for the use of a standard flush fitting. If you want flush fittings on a thin solid hull, it will be necessary to lay up fiberglass on the inside of the hull, in effect building a fiberglass backing block under the seacock at least as thick as the hull skin—preferably thicker.

Ideally, the buildup should cover an area of at least a foot square, and should consist of alternating layers of mat and roving. There is some risk of distorting the hull locally from the heat of laying up this fairly large patch, so it is best done a few layers at a time. Unless wax-free laminating resin is used, cured layers should be sanded and washed with acetone before adding additional laminate.

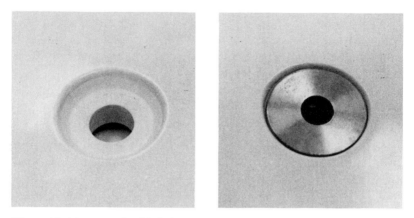

The molded-in recess in this balsa-cored hull is designed to take an American-style flush fitting.

Once the backing block is laid up, you can cut the mortise for the flush fitting using the same method described for cored hulls.

Other Solutions

Installing the typical flush through-hull fitting is a big job. A much more easily installed flush fitting is made in Europe, but it does not appear to be available in this country. The European fitting has a relatively small flange, and the edges of the flange are neither rounded like a surface mount fitting, nor beveled on the underside like the typical flush fitting; instead, the edges are square-sided. This means that cutting a mortise is a simple, one-step operation, involving only a large spade bit or a hole saw and chisel to cut and finish the recess. In addition, the flange of the European-type fitting is fairly thin, so the mortise depth is shallow, allowing installation in fairly thin fiberglass hulls without heavy reinforcing on the inside of the hull.

If your hull is thick enough, or if you are willing to do a little more work on the inside of the boat to locally strengthen the hull, you can recess a through-hull designed for surface mounting, using the same method required for the European-type fitting. Be sure to make the mortise slightly deeper than the flange thickness, and coat the inside of the mortise with a layer of resin to prevent any wicking of water in the laminate.

When installing any through-hull, you should relieve the

edge of hole for the stem of the fitting. This rounded area will hold enough bedding compound to keep the fitting from leaking. Without it, it is easy to squeeze out all the compound under the fitting during installation, particularly if the fitting is screwed into the seacock rather than screwing the seacock onto the through-hull fitting.

Once the fitting is installed, trowel the edges of the mortise with epoxy putty to smooth the transition between hull and through-hull fitting. Sand the putty smooth, touch up any voids, and prime with epoxy primer. Then wet sand to smooth the area and apply bottom paint.

*   *   *

Several rules apply when recessing fittings, whether you use special flush fittings or regular surface-mount through-hulls:

• The depth of the mortise should not exceed half the thickness of the hull unless the inside of the hull is reinforced.

• Backing blocks are essential on the inside of the hull to help distribute load.

• No core material should be left exposed in cored hulls.

If you cannot meet these conditions, you should fair in the fitting rather than recessing it.

Whichever method you choose, reducing the drag of through-hull fittings is only the first step in creating a low-resistance bottom. It can be a reasonably simple project if you take the short course—fairing in—but can quickly develop into a time-consuming job if you choose to recess the fittings flush with the surface of the hull.

Don't be disappointed if you don't notice an immediate improvement in the performance of your boat, since we are talking about a relatively small reduction in drag. However, if you combine reducing through-hull drag with other improvements, such as careful attention to the propeller installation and the application of bottom paint, you will be well on the way to a noticeable improvement in performance.

5

Electrical and Electronic Projects

UPGRADING THE 12-VOLT SYSTEM

The age of marine electronics has been a boon to sailors; sophisticated performance instruments, accurate position-finding equipment, and compact and powerful radio transceivers cost a fraction of the price of similar equipment just a few years ago. Unfortunately, if your boat is more than a few years old, its electrical system may be woefully inadequate for the demands of today's abundant and inexpensive electrical gear.

It is not that the power requirements of modern electronics are excessive. In fact, they are downright miserly in that respect compared to their counterparts of a few years ago. The problem is that most production boats lack the electrical panel space and the built-in wiring for the expansion of the system beyond just the basics. If your boat has only a six-circuit system, you simply have no space for expansion within the existing system after you have designated circuits for cabin lights, running lights, anchor light, bilge pump, VHF radio, and depth finder.

The temptation to pigtail new equipment onto existing circuits is overwhelming. After all, what you really want to do is to get your new piece of equipment up and running quickly, even if it has to get power from the cabin-light circuit.

As pervasive as that attitude is, it is a poor approach to take to low-voltage wiring. Improper 12-volt wiring can lower a boat's resale value, lead to reduced performance of the electronic equipment, make troubleshooting all but impossible, and could even cause a fire.

Direct Connections

The manufacturers of many add-on electrical devices such as VHF radios and Loran sets have not helped the situation, stressing that their products should be wired directly to the battery terminals, bypassing the boat's electrical distribution system. By specifying the conductor size and a direct connection to the battery, manufacturers guarantee that their electronics will have a clean, low-resistance path to power, independent of the shortcomings of the rest of the electrical system. In addition, a direct connection to the battery allows the battery to serve as a large capacitor; thus protecting electronics from voltage fluctuations caused by the other components of the electrical system, such as an autopilot or an old-fashioned generator.

Direct connections to the battery frequently result in excessive wiring runs and an indecipherable rat's nest of wire around the battery terminals. Direct connections also mean that if you forget to turn off the VHF when you leave the boat, you could return a week later to find dead batteries, even if you remembered to throw the master switch.

The only items you should consider wiring directly to the battery are an electric bilge pump and a voltmeter for battery testing. If wired directly, the bilge pump must be provided with its own fuse or circuit breaker, and a separate switch panel. Many bilge-pump manufacturers sell small, fused bilge-pump panels specifically for this type of installation. A separate panel allows you to leave the bilge pump on "automatic," even with the rest of the electrical system shut down (as it should be when you are not on the boat).

When deciding how to wire a new piece of gear, the safest approach is to call the service department of the manufacturer of the item, telling them that you want to wire the item through the boat's distribution system rather than directly to the battery, and ask if there are any particular precautions that should be taken to avoid damage from voltage spike. The service department electrician may want to know what generator or alternator you have, and may want to know what other electronics you have on the boat. He may suggest noise suppressors on the alternator output or the power feed to the individual piece of gear.

A New Distribution Panel

Having decided against wiring direct connections to your battery, you will probably discover that your electrical panel has no circuits left to use. The time may have come to expand your electrical system.

In the past few years, distribution panels using circuit breakers have largely replaced switch-and-fuse electrical panels on most boats over 30 feet. While a circuit-breaker panel is about twice as expensive as a fuse panel, as a rule, a breaker panel is easier to install and maintain.

The modern DC circuit breaker is reliable and should provide trouble-free service for a long time. While both thermal and magnetic/hydraulic breakers are suited for marine use, the majority of ready-made electrical panels use Airpax magnetic/ hydraulic breakers.

If your electrical panel consists of a simple fuse and switch panel, or if you are out of open circuits and you plan to add electronic gear, you should consider upgrading your electrical system with a new distribution panel containing enough circuits for present and future installations. The 25-foot cruising boat with Loran, VHF, and full instrumentation is becoming the rule rather than the exception, so don't underestimate your needs.

Ready-made distribution panels using circuit breakers come in just about every imaginable size, shape, and capacity; from simple six-circuit panels, similar to the familiar switch and fuse panels, to AC/DC master panels that look like something out of a battleship. What you should buy depends as much on the mounting space available as it does on the demands you will make on the electrical system.

Protecting the Electrical Panel

This is also the time to consider moving the electrical panel. The panel should be in a convenient location that is protected from spray and accidental bumps. The galley area is generally a poor location for any electrical installation. Cooking steam can accelerate corrosion, and a galley fire might keep you from shutting down the system when you need to. Under the bridgedeck might seem like a good location, but water pouring down the companionway could wipe out the system in an instant.

Installing a new distribution panel provides a good opportunity to straighten out a rat's nest of wiring like this.

If the panel is exposed, but moving it to another location is impractical, you should build a protective cover for the panel. This can be as simple as a wood frame, a length of piano hinge, and a piece of clear acrylic or polycarbonate plastic for a cover.

Good locations for the electrical panel include the navigation station in larger boats, and at the forward end of a quarterberth or above and behind a settee in a smaller boat. If the panel is mounted in the navigation station, make sure that the navigator will not have to lean against the panel on one tack or the other.

Wiring Logic

If you are moving the panel, be sure that there will be adequate depth behind the panel (about five inches behind the face), and that it is physically possible to make the wiring runs to the new location. You must also consider whether a change in location will require going to a heavier gauge of wire for the leads from the battery to the panel. In general, moving any distribution panel more complicated than a six-circuit board will be a major project, and may be more trouble than it is worth unless the present location is totally unacceptable.

Whether you are replacing wiring or expanding the system, don't unhook any existing wire without labeling it clearly. Stick-on numbered labels are available at any electronics store. Of course, when using numbered labels, you must keep a master key to the system.

To decide the number of circuits you will need, write down every item of electrical equipment you might add while you own the boat. A well-equipped cruiser can easily fill a dozen circuits unless you go the route of extreme simplicity.

Every piece of permanently installed electronic communication and navigation equipment (VHF, Loran, depth sounder, and SatNav, for example) should have its own circuit. Lumping all these into one circuit labelled "electronics" is asking for trouble. Even though many compact electronics are designed to run off internal batteries as well as the boat's 12-volt system, consider making provision for attaching them to the normal electrical system in case the built-in batteries die.

No circuit using the regular distribution panel should be rated at more than 20 amps. Unless you have an electric anchor windlass, the only circuit that might approach this demand is the cabin lighting circuit. On larger boats, the standard practice is to divide the cabin lighting into two circuits, so that a failure in one will not leave the boat in the dark. If you divide the lighting, try to do so in a logical fashion that both minimizes wire runs and equally divides the current demand.

How Is Your Old Wiring?

Replacing or adding to your electrical panel provides a good opportunity to examine the rest of the wiring. A common cause of poor electrical system performance is corroded terminal connections. Mechanical crimp connections are just about universal on boats, as they are in automobiles. The common crimp terminal, however, leaves exposed a certain amount of copper wire which protrudes through the terminal after it is crimped. The combination of warm salty air, electrical current, and the inevitable mixture of metals in the electrical system often produces a fair amount of copper salts on the terminals or connections, causing increased resistance and voltage drop, generally reducing electrical system performance. We'll deal with the solutions to these problems later in this chapter.

Undersize wiring also reduces system efficiency. You can easily calculate the wire gauge needed for any circuit using the table on page 167 of Volume 3, *Maintenance and Repairs*. A simpler approach, however, is to settle on the largest size conductor you will need for any individual circuit (other than high-amperage circuits like an electrical windlass or engine starter), and use that size conductor for all the circuits. Using slightly oversize wire will reduce the voltage drop in long runs and give you enough wire capacity to pigtail on later if necessary.

What Gauge Wire?

For all practical purposes, 12-gauge wire can be used for individual 12-volt circuits which will not have loads over 20 amps. Although the voltage drop will vary with the length of the wire run for the circuit, 12-gauge wire will keep the loss to acceptable levels for any wire run on boats up to about 45 feet long. This does not include wire runs to the masthead for strobes or running lights, which may require heavier wiring.

Using a single gauge of wire simplifies wire and connector buying, and your electronics will appreciate the lower voltage drop associated with heavier wiring. The extra cost of heavier wire is nominal, and the savings from buying connectors in bulk rather than in packages of five should be substantial.

Tinned Wire

While the ordinary two-conductor stranded wire in the grey vinyl jacket is used almost universally, corrosion in the system will be greatly reduced if tinned copper wiring is used instead. Each individual strand of this wire is tin coated in the manufacturing process. Since most crimp connectors are tin-plated copper, galvanic action between the surface of the wire and the connector is minimized by the use of tinned wire, and connectors will stay electrically cleaner for a longer period of time.

Another advantage of most tinned wire is that the conductors are twisted around each other inside the vinyl outer jacket. This reduces the magnetic field that might otherwise be created by the conductors, minimizing the effect on the ship's compass or radio direction finder.

Tinned wire is slightly more expensive than plain copper wire, and is much harder to come by. It is worth the search, however. You won't be able to get tinned copper wire at the local auto parts store, although a good electronics store can order it for you. An excellent wire of this specification is Alpha 1892, made by Alpha Wire Corporation (Elizabeth, NJ 07207). This wire has the further advantage of meeting ABYC standards for type 3 wire, meaning that the large number of strands allow it to be used in wiring subject to frequent flexing. The cost is about $40 per 100 feet.

Color Coding

When adding wiring to an existing system, keep the color coding of the new wiring consistent with what you already have. Only white or black should be used for the grounded (negative) conductor. If your electrical system uses two conductor wiring with white and black conductors, like house wiring, carefully trace the existing wire to ascertain the proper polarity. The most common practice in systems that do not use ABYC color-coding is to use two conductor wiring with conductors coded red (positive) and black (negative).

To keep wiring neat and workmanlike, always use PVC-jacketed two-conductor wiring. Strip the outer jacket back only as far as is necessary when making connections, since it provides extra protection against wear. Nylon cable ties are cheap and allow you to bundle the wire into neat runs.

Don't run wire through the bilge. It will be more work to lead wiring behind settee fronts or through bulkheads, but even without exposed connections, wiring does not belong where it can get wet.

Primary Wiring

A potential problem in expanding the small boat's electrical system is that the primary wiring from the battery selector switch to the panel may not be heavy enough for the electrical demands of a larger system. If there is a master DC breaker in the panel, the primary conductor from the battery to the master

The back of a well-organized distribution panel, ready for installation. Note the heavy primary wiring from the ammeter to each bank of circuit breakers, and the neatly bundled leads from the breakers for each circuit. Light-gauge wiring is for LED status-indicator lights.

breaker must be rated to carry at least as much current as the capacity of the breaker. If there is no master breaker, the primary panel wiring should be heavy enough to carry the entire electrical system load if every current-demanding item on the boat were on at once.

In practice, 6-gauge primary wiring allows an adequate safety margin on the typical boat up to about 45 feet long, with a total instantaneous load (everything on) of 50 amps. This does not include the cables to the engine starter, which must never take power through the distribution panel, and which must have heavier wire to cope with the tremendous load of a starter motor.

Even outboard-powered boats benefit from heavy primary wiring. A 25-footer with a single battery and no on-board charging capability should still have a master disconnect switch if there is more to the electrical system than an electric bilge pump. The wiring between battery, switch, and panel should be 10 gauge or heavier—even in this simple installation. If the outboard has battery-charging capability, go to the same gauge primary wiring used in inboard installations. There is no such thing as wiring that is too heavy for the job.

Panel Mechanics

Installation of an additional distribution panel should be straightforward, provided there is room to consider it in the first place. Power is taken to the new panel (which should be in close proximity to the old one, if possible) via a short jumper from the positive feed to the existing panel. The jumper to the new panel should be the same gauge as the feeder to the old panel, providing the old feeder is heavy enough for the demands of the expanded system. If it is necessary to add another negative buss for the additional circuits, a similar jumper can be made from the existing negative buss to the new one.

In a simple electrical system, the individual positive leads can be connected directly to their circuit breakers or switches. In complex systems—anything more than eight circuits—the wiring will be neater if the positive conductors for each circuit are first led to barrier strips. A short, carefully bundled harness can be made up to lead from the barrier strip to the back of the panel.

Note that this will increase the number of connections, a violation of basic principle. It should therefore only be done in larger boats, where the complexity of wiring behind the panel would produce a rat's nest, and where the electrical panel is located away from any spray. Even on a dry boat, these connections—and every connection—should be sprayed with a water-displacing lubricant such as CRC or WD-40 after all connections are made. Be sure that whatever spray you use is made to be used on electrical connections, as some water-displacing sprays are slightly conductive.

Good access to the back of the panel is important. The depth behind the panel can be increased, if necessary, by mounting the panel on a wooden frame. Access will be even better if the panel is hinged like the door of a locker. A piece of piano hinge is ideal for this application. Make sure that you leave enough slack in the wiring to allow you to open the hinged panel completely, and make sure there is enough space behind the panel to accommodate the extra length of wire required in this type of installation. This is where neat wiring really pays off.

There is nothing particularly difficult about wiring, but it is one of the most time-consuming projects you can tackle. For this reason, expanding or replacing the electrical system is an ideal winter project. This summer, figure out what your electrical needs really are, and examine your existing system in the light of everyday use.

The complete boatowner has many skills. He is a rigger, a carpenter, a painter, a plumber, and an electrician. He is an engineer, a mechanic, a meteorologist, and a sailmaker. And oh yes, he is even a sailor sometimes—when he has time off from his other jobs.

SYSTEM MONITOR INSTALLATION

When expanding your electrical system, consider adding a voltmeter for battery testing and an ammeter to monitor power consumption. These meters are often included in the more expensive ready-made panels, but they can also be purchased as separate units to match most existing panels.

Alternatively, you can make up your own voltmeter-ammeter panels by using meters purchased from an electrical supply house. You will need a 0-50 amp DC ammeter and a 0-15 or 8-16 volt DC voltmeter. A voltmeter reading from 8 to 16 volts with an expanded scale and suppressed zero is the easiest to read for battery testing, but it may be harder to find than a 0-15 volt unit. We have used a Simpson 9570 voltmeter and a Simpson 2530 ammeter with good results.

The larger the meter faces are, the easier they will be to read. The more expensive they are, the more accurate they will be. A cheap voltmeter may be too inaccurate for battery testing. A suitable voltmeter and ammeter will each cost about $30 to $40.

The ammeter will be either direct reading or remote reading, which requires an external shunt. Direct-reading ammeters are wired into the positive primary wire from the battery selector switch to the panel. A remote-reading ammeter with an external shunt may be mounted at any convenient location. The shunt is wired into the primary positive lead, and light-gauge wires are led from the shunt to the meter. An ammeter wired in this fashion will show the total amperage being used, and will help you to control your power consumption. It will not show minute power leakage.

To finish the voltmeter testing circuit, you need a single-pole, double-throw switch with "off" in the center position. Lead a wire from the positive terminal of each battery to one of the terminals on each end of the switch. In most switches of this specification, there are three terminals on the back. For our purposes, consider the center one as the feed to the positive side of the voltmeter, and the two outer terminals as the input from the positive side of each battery.

Make up a short jumper from the center switch terminal to the positive terminal of the voltmeter. Take another wire from the negative post of either battery to the negative terminal of the voltmeter. When buying a switch for this use, be sure you understand which terminal on the back serves which function; not all switch terminals are set up the same way.

Finally, you must protect each of the positive leads from the battery to the test switch with an in-line fuse holder, which you can also get from an electronics store. A 5-amp glass fuse is more than enough, since the meter does not really draw anything. The fuses, which should be placed close the battery, serve to protect the wires to the meter in the event of a short.

A QUICK AND EASY SOLDERING LESSON

Nine times out of ten, when there is an electrical problem on a boat, the problem lies neither in the appliance nor in the wiring. Most often the problem is a poor connection.

The fatalistic boat owner with recurrent electrical problems is apt to shrug off his problems with the popular adage, "Seawater and electricity don't mix." The more pragmatic skipper goes out and spends $10 on a soldering iron and cures his problem once and for all.

Soldering is so easy to learn and the equipment so inexpensive, it is hard to imagine why anyone—especially on a boat—would want to make their electrical connections any other way. Here is what you need to get started.

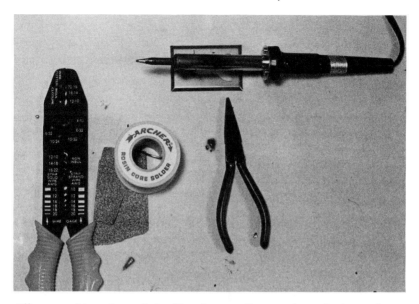

All you need to make perfect soldered connections: a wire stripping tool, sandpaper, pliers, rosin-core solder and a 40 watt soldering iron.

The Soldering Iron

Soldering irons come in all sizes and with a variety of tips, each designed for different soldering tasks. Generally, irons are classified by wattage. The smaller wattage irons, in the 25- to 30-watt range, are useful for component work only. They tend to have small pointed tips best suited for very fine work. Transistors and other electrical components are easily damaged by using hotter irons with tips that radiate heat in too wide an area.

The hottest soldering irons, often rated 200 watts or more, are used mainly for structural work, such as soldering plumbing connections. These irons have limited application on a boat, due to the relatively small gauge wire used in 12-volt circuitry.

A 40-watt soldering iron is perfectly adequate for just about all marine soldering, except perhaps on engine starter wiring or on connections between the battery and an electric windlass. A 40-watt iron with a small tip will do a good job on most fine soldering jobs, but it still puts out enough heat with a larger tip to solder a 10-gauge wire connection.

When buying a soldering iron, look for two things. Make

sure it bears an Underwriter's Laboratory seal of approval and that it features an interchangeable tip. Radio Shack and Sears offer a good selection of irons for less than $15. For a few dollars more, you can buy a dual-setting iron in a kit which includes a stand, a roll of solder, needle-nose pliers and even a wire stripping and crimping tool.

Several manufacturers also sell rechargeable soldering irons that will last for several weeks of light use between charges.

The Right Solder for the Job

Solder consists of tin and lead in different amounts. A 50:50 alloy, which melts at 425 degrees F, is a bit stronger than the 60:40 (lead to tin) alloy, which melts at 371 degrees. Obviously, joints or connections that would benefit from the stronger solder bond ought to be made with the 50:50 alloy.

Another difference between solders is the kind of flux, or core, they contain. Never use acid flux or acid-core solder; the proper solder for all electrical work is rosin-core solder.

Getting Started

Besides solder and an iron, you will need a stand for the soldering iron, a damp rag or sponge, a stripping tool and some sandpaper or steel wool. Make sure all the copper surfaces are bright and shiny before starting any soldering. A stripping tool is essential for removing insulation without damaging the wire underneath, especially for the multistrand wire most commonly used in 12-volt marine applications.

Once the iron is hot, the first step is to tin the tip. Tinning is simply spreading a thin layer of solder on the tip, which will make sure no impurities are transferred from the tip to the joint. Tinning also ensures that a maximum amount of heat is transferred from the iron to the joint. Periodically during the job you may have to freshen the tinning. If the tip gets dark or burned-looking, simply wipe the tip clean while it is hot with the sponge or damp rag and reapply a small amount of solder. A properly tinned tip, like a properly soldered piece of work, always will look bright and silvery.

If the tip is dirty and crusty, clean it thoroughly with fine sandpaper, steel wool or emery cloth before you heat the iron.

Oxides can prevent the solder from adhering properly to a new joint. Spreading some soldering paste on the tip before it is heated will help prevent oxides from forming, but this step is not usually necessary.

Make sure the joint is mechanically sound before soldering takes place. Solder, after all, is not intended to give strength to the joint or connection. Its main purpose is to seal the connection from moisture and dirt that will impede the flow of electricity.

Soldering a Joint

The most difficult aspect of soldering is organizing the work. You need one hand to hold the iron, and another to hold the work. So how do you hold the solder? It is helpful to have a vise or clamp to hold the work. Another method is to put the roll of solder on the table, unwind a couple of turns, bend over the top last few inches of the solder, and simply ease the joint and iron up to the solder when the work is heated.

The most important thing to remember about soldering is to always heat the work, not the solder. If you drip hot solder onto a cold joint, the connection is likely to fail just as quickly as if it had never been soldered. Cold-soldered joints, as these are called, are easily spotted by their dull, lumpy appearance. A good, hot-soldered joint is shiny and smooth.

Since heat rises, you will spend less time waiting for the work to heat up if you can get the iron directly under the piece to be soldered. When you think the connection is hot enough, lightly touch the solder to the top of the work. The solder should flow easily into the joint, as if the joint were sucking up the solder. Flow on just enough solder so that all surfaces are lightly covered. Don't try to lump on large amounts of solder. Remove the solder and keep the iron on the joint for a few seconds longer to make sure the solder spreads evenly into all the nooks and crannies of the connection. Keep the joint still until it cools.

After a joint or connection has been soldered, it should be protected from the elements and from chafing. Good-quality cloth electrician's tape followed by a thin, even layer of silicone, will protect a joint both from chafe and moisture.

Another good protective barrier can be made with heat-shrink tubing, which can be purchased in most electrical supply houses. Cut the tubing and slide it over one of the wires before making the joint. After soldering, slide the tubing over the connection and use a hair dryer to shrink-wrap the connection.

Two Good Electrical Connections

A soldered connection is only as good as its mechanical bonding. The most common method of joining two wires together is to twist the ends together, a joint that is called a rat-tail joint. While this is a good joint in home wiring where it is covered with a wire nut and placed in a junction box, the rat-tail joint is not the best joint to use in the damp marine environment. The joint is so large that it is hard to solder properly, and it is a tough connection to insulate properly with tape or other covering.

A far better joint is the modified Western Union splice. It creates a stronger mechanical bond, lies flat for easy insulating and is compact for quick and thorough soldering. This elegant joint is made by wrapping the end of each wire around the other wire. After making several turns with each end, firmly pull both wires to draw the knotted ends together as tightly as possible. Use a pair of pliers to keep the turns tight, if necessary, as the joint is being made.

The Western Union splice (it is called a modified Western Union joint when you use multistrand wire, instead of a solid copper conductor) is good for joining any two wires together, even if the wires are of different diameter. One common application is when adding an in-line fuse.

Another equally useful and classy joint is the T-splice, also called a knotted tap splice. After stripping away the insulation in the middle of the wire to be tapped, take a turn around it with the T-wire. Next, bring the T-wire around itself as close to the tapped wire as possible. Resume wrapping—this time on the other side of the T-wire from the original wrap. These wraps, you will note, go around in the opposite direction from the original turn. Make sure the wraps are tight. The T-wire should not move easily along the tapped wire.

This splice is useful any time you want to tap into an existing line rather than run a new lead all the way back to the control panel or power source. One application might be in adding a new light to an existing cabin-light circuit. As always, make sure

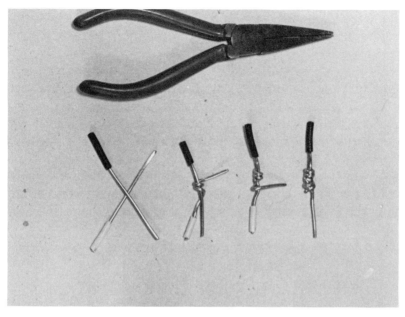

Four steps to a Western Union splice: Cross wires. Make several turns around the standing part of one wire, then wrap the remaining lead over the remaining standing wire. Pull the wires to make sure the joint is as tight as possible. Note that solid copper wire is used in these photo as a visual aide. In most 12-volt applications, the proper wiring is multistrand copper.

the connection is adequately insulated, that the circuit is adequately fused, and that the wire is of adequate gauge to handle the electrical load.

Other Connections

Crimp-on connectors have many uses on a boat, but they should be soldered as well as crimped. The best crimp connectors have metal sleeves and can be purchased at any good chandlery or electrical supply house. Crimp-on connectors with plastic sleeves make soldering difficult, but the plastic may be cut off to expose the metal sleeve. Make sure the sleeve is the correct size— just slightly larger than the diameter of the wire. Crimp the sleeve twice with a crimping tool, then heat the sleeve with the soldering iron and add solder. Allow the sleeve to drink up as much solder as it will hold. If you slip a piece of shrink tubing on the wire before crimping, you can slide it over the sleeve after soldering for a perfectly protected connection.

*   *   *

Taking a few minutes to learn proper soldering techniques can save hours when adding a new electronic component or upgrading the electrical system. Perhaps the best reason, however, for taking the time to make good connections is that when the inevitable problem does occur, you will not have to spend time searching out and testing every splice in the system. If you are confident that your connections are sound, you can concentrate your troubleshooting on more likely sources of the problem.

BUILD A CUSTOM MULTIFUNCTION ALARM SYSTEM

Have you ever gotten up at 3 a.m. to find six inches of cold water over the cabin sole? If you have, then you already know the value of a good bilge alarm. A good alarm system does not cost much, is very reliable, and will give you a feeling of security whether at anchor or underway. Some insurance companies will even lower your rate if an alarm system is installed. The system shown here can be put in by anyone who can solder a wire and find the local Radio Shack store.

The size and complexity of your system depends on the size of the boat and the degree of sophistication you desire. A small auxiliary sailboat will generally need no more than a high-water alarm and a set of engine sensors. A fifty-foot charter vessel with a separate engine room and several staterooms might have a bilge alarm for each area, fire sensors for the engine room and galley, smoke detectors, low-oil and hot-engine sensors on the engines, and possibly, a circuit for the keel cooler or transmission-oil level. Commercial boats often alarm their hydraulics and refrigeration systems as well.

There are many types of switches, bells, and whistles that might be used to advantage, but the ones mentioned here have all proven to be reliable in service. Reliability is the aim, since an alarm that does not work could be dangerous if it lulls you into a false sense of security.

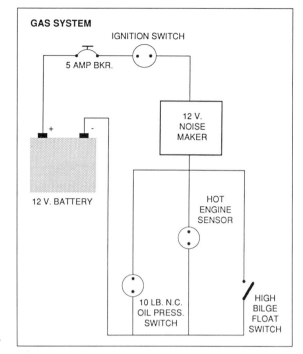

GAS SYSTEM

IGNITION SWITCH

5 AMP BKR.

12 V.
NOISE
MAKER

+ -

12 V. BATTERY

HOT
ENGINE
SENSOR

10 LB. N.C.
OIL PRESS.
SWITCH

HIGH
BILGE
FLOAT
SWITCH

Figure 5-1A.

The noise-making part of the unit must be loud enough to awaken you from a sound sleep, but not so loud that it interferes with orders or instructions. A simple 12-volt bell about four inches in diameter will provide more than enough volume for any boat up to about sixty feet in length. Larger boats might need two bells to fully cover the area. If only one bell is to be used, locate it in an open central area. Bells should be able to be heard from a fair distance away from the boat; you may not be aboard when a problem occurs, but the bell may alert a passerby or a passing vessel to the problem.

For most boats up to about thirty feet, the entire package consists of the bell, a float switch for the bilges, and a low-oil and high-temperature sensor kit for the engine. **Figures 5-1A** and **5-1B** show this simple system for both gasoline and diesel engines. It is most suitable for boats that are used infrequently; long-distance cruisers need more protection.

Family cruisers should consider the schematic shown in **Figure 5-2**. Don't be put off by its apparent complexity. Most of

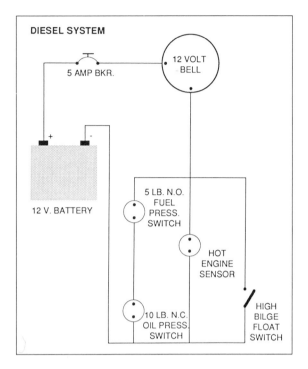

Figure 5-1B.

it can be built on a piece of perforated board just a few inches square. The lights in this system tell you what sensor has found something wrong without having to visually check every compartment and gauge. The test switches allow you to test the bulbs and to test the circuits to make sure that the system is in working order. The lights and test switches could be mounted near the engine controls, but if this proves inconvenient, they may be placed anywhere they can be seen easily. Some charter boats even have a second set in the captain's cabin.

Float Switches

When deciding where you will mount your high-bilge alarm (float) switches, it helps to know how they are constructed. Generally, they contain a glass vial that is partially filled with mercury, with two metal contacts imbedded in one end. Two wires are attached to the contacts and the vial is cast into a block of foam. The foam block is then sealed into a plastic case that is fitted with a pivot at one end. In use, the switch is set so that the mercury falls to the end of the tube. As bilge water rises, the foam block floats, letting the mercury flow back to the contacts, completing the circuit, and thus ringing the bell.

Float switches that are mounted athwartships may flop around while the boat is heeled and give false indications. They can also be set off when a slight amount of water sloshes around in a shallow bilge. For this reason, place them facing fore and aft in the bilge sump, and mount them two or three inches above the bilge-pump float switch. If your boat has a flat, shallow bilge, you should give plenty of thought to the location selected. You may want to do a little experimenting before permanently mounting the switch.

Fire Sensors

A fire sensor is inexpensive and reliable. It is a "normally open" thermal switch, that closes at a temperature of about 150 degrees Fahrenheit, and will re-open when the temperature goes down. You can find them in most of the larger marine stores around the country. The switches are small and unobtrusive, but must be placed in exactly the right spot to do their job.

Around the galley, they should be placed so that they will not be affected by normal cooking heat, but will be set off by a fire before it gets out of control. Mounting sensors in the engine compartment requires some trial and error since virtually all of the engine parts are hotter than the sensor will tolerate. The easiest way to find the proper location is to leave the leads long enough to reach anywhere in the compartment, and then temporarily tape the switch to its intended location during a sea trial. When you find a suitable location, you can cut the wires to length and mount the sensor.

Engine Alarm Sensors

Alarm sensors for oil pressure and overheating are also inexpensive. Marine engine dealers can supply you with the type you need for your engine. Hot-engine sensors are installed into an existing port in the engine's cooling-water jacket; low-oil pressure sensors are tapped into the oil-pressure line, usually directly onto the engine where the oil-pressure gauge is taken off.

Contact your dealer or manufacturer for an exact takeoff point.

A fuel-pressure cutoff switch is shown in the schematics. It is used because the engine-oil pressure is at zero when the engines are stopped, which would otherwise allow the engine-oil alarm to sound continuously. Take a close look at the schematics as they relate to the fuel-pressure and engine-oil pressure switches. Notice that the fuel-line switch is a five-pound normally open type, while the oil-pressure switch is a ten-pound normally closed type.

In diesel installations, the fuel switch is installed in the fuel return line, not the high-pressure line leading to the injectors. If you hook it up wrong, you can plan on a trip to your local dealer to buy another switch. If in doubt, check with your mechanic.

If you have a gasoline engine, no fuel switch is used. You will have to turn the engine alarm on and off with either the ignition

Figure 5-2.

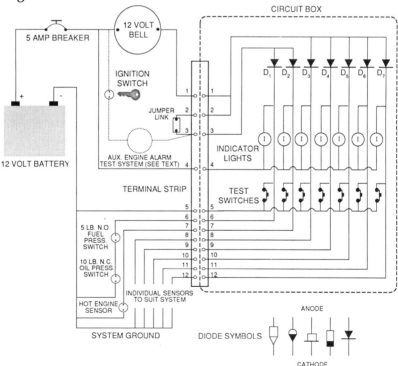

key or another switch. In operation, the alarm will ring from the time you turn on the key, until the engine-oil pressure comes up past ten pounds. This is usually not more than five or ten seconds, but it serves as a good test of the engine sensors at every start up. A diesel system will ring from the time the fuel pressure reaches five pounds until the engine-oil pressure reaches ten pounds. Depending on your engine, this can be just one short ring, or may last for about thirty seconds.

Diodes

Diodes operate as electrical check valves. They allow current to flow in one direction only. Because of this, they must be installed in the circuit exactly as shown, with the cathode end connected to the indicator light. To help those not versed in electronics, a drawing of several common diode shapes has been included in the main schematic in Figure 5-2. A typical symbol for a diode is included for reference. The diodes used may have a voltage rating of any value over ten amps. For cruising, you might want to carry two or three spare diodes on the boat just in case something goes wrong far from home.

Lights, Switches, and Terminal Strips

The indicator lights shown in the schematic are 12-volt types, of any available size and style. The panel will be somewhat easier to work on if the bulbs can be replaced from the front of the panel. Large light fixtures with high-wattage bulbs will tend to blind you at night, and may require you to increase the wire size, breaker rating, and diode amp rating.

The test switches are small, normally open push-button types, available from Radio Shack in blister packs of five. Their only drawback is that they are so small that you may have trouble holding them for soldering or mounting.

Terminal strips are long thin strips of plastic that have two rows of contact points down their length. Each set of contacts is shorted together with a small strip of metal. They are used to make temporary attachments, and for items that may need to be removed from time to time. We are using one on the system so that you will be able to make the test box at one time, and wire the boat at a later date.

Circuit Description

Although the schematic in Figure 5-2 may look complex, it is really quite simple. Let's take an electrical walk through it and see how it functions. For ease of explanation we will concern ourselves with just one of the sensors, since the entire alarm box is simply a series of identical circuits gathered together to operate a single bell.

Starting at the battery, power for the alarm is taken directly off the battery post, not the battery switch. (You will want your alarms to work regardless of whether the master switch is on or off.) After it leaves the battery terminal, the wire goes to one terminal of a 5-amp DC breaker. The breaker is there to protect the wire from burning if a short develops in the circuit. A fuse could also be used, but you must carry spares, and they do not tell you when they are blown. Mount the breaker as close to the

Figure 5-3.

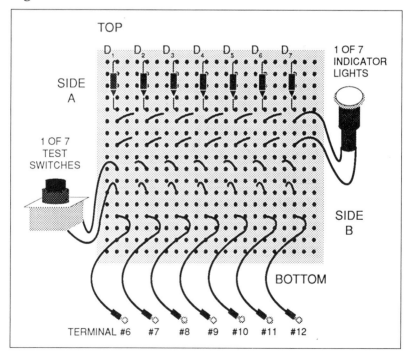

battery as possible. The other terminal of the breaker is connected to one side of the bell, while the other bell terminal is connected to terminal #1 of the terminal strip. The other side of the terminal #1 is connected to the anodes of all of the diodes in the box (except the engine sensors which we will discuss later).

The cathode sides of each diode are connected to one side of an indicator light, one side of a test switch, and to the alarm sensors. The other side of the sensor is attached to the negative side of the battery.

When a sensor switch closes, it connects the negative side of the battery to the cathode side of the diode. It also connects one side of the indicator light to the negative side of the battery, causing the light to glow.

The test switches work in just the same way, except that they contact the negative side of the battery by way of terminal #5. All of the indicator lights have their positive leads going to terminal

Figure 5-4.

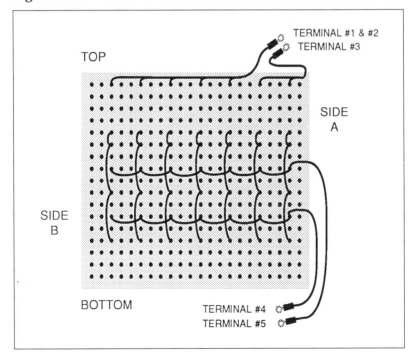

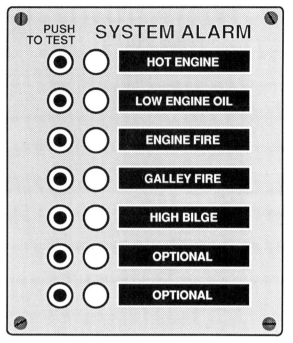

Figure 5-5.

#4, which is connected to the positive side of the circuit breaker.

Now we come to the one problem that might be encountered. Note the jumper between terminal #2 and #3? It must be there because some boats have their fuel tanks mounted higher than the engines. This puts pressure into the fuel system when the tanks are full, and can sometimes hold the fuel-pressure switch in the open position. This causes the low-oil alarm to sound whenever the engine is not running. The only way to cure the problem is to install another bell. The second bell is shown dotted in the schematic. It, in effect, creates two separate alarm systems, one of them taking its power from the ignition switch when the engine is running.

Wiring

All wiring used in the alarm system should be at least 16-gauge stranded copper. Never use solid wire in a boat. The insulation should be capable of withstanding at least 600 volts, and a temperature of 95 degrees C. Use splices in your wire only where you must, and solder all connections and terminals with rosin-core solder as outlined earlier in this chapter.

Everything inside of the dotted line in Figure 5-2 is fitted into a small plastic box, with the lights and test switches mounted on the cover. Be sure to leave enough wire between the switches and lights, and the cover, so that the circuit board can easily be removed to get at the parts inside. If you like, you can mount the lights and test switches near the instruments, and just mount the diodes on a piece of board in the box. Place a piece of sponge rubber padding on top and below the circuit board before you mount it in the box. This will stop the board from rattling and guarantee that the parts on the board will not touch the lights or switches and short something out.

Drawings of the front and back of the circuit board are shown in **Figures 5-3** and **5-4**, with the completed alarm box shown in **Figure 5-5**. The board itself is made of a small section cut from a perforated board sold by Radio Shack. You need only poke the leads of the diode through the holes and hook them together as

---

Figure 5-6. Alarm System Trouble-Shooting Guide

Nothing is happening anywhere in the system.	- Main breaker tripped or fuse blown. - Ground wire disconnected.
All lights go on when any sensor is grounded.	- Diodes were installed in the board backward.
Engine alarms do not work.	- Jumper link missing between Terminals #2 and #3. - Wire missing between Terminals #1 and #2 inside of alarm box. - Ignition switch not on (some installations).
One alarm rings all of the time.	- Bad or improperly mounted sensor. - Sensor wire shorted to ground (neg.) between terminal and sensor. - Stuck or shorted test switch.
Alarm rings but light will not light.	- Missing or burned out bulb. - Power not run to Terminal #4.
Breaker keeps tripping.	- Short between Terminals #4 and #5. - Short somewhere between breaker and Terminal #4.

shown to form the circuits. Figure 5-5 shows one light and one switch connected to the circuit board. The other lights and switches have been omitted for clarity, but you can see the stubs of the wires where they attach.

When you are soldering the parts together, try not to use too much heat on the diodes. Some types can be rather sensitive to high temperatures, and might roll over and die if subjected to excess heat. Your solder joints should look clean and shiny. If they look granular or dull, you should do them over.

* * *

Once your alarm system is installed and functioning, it should be trouble-free for many years. Just in case, however, you can make a photocopy of the trouble-shooting guide in **Figure 5-6** to keep with your other ship's papers. Or better yet, keep the entire *Practical Sailor Library* on the shelf above the settee. You never know when you might want to start on a new project.

INSTALL AN ENGINE HOUR METER

Knowing when to do preventive maintenance on your auxiliary engine can be just as important as knowing what to do and how to do it. A conscientious boatowner may simply change the engine oil twice a year, once at the middle of the season and again at the end. But is this enough? And how often should the air and fuel filters be changed? How do you know when your valves need adjusting, or that it is time for a total overhaul? And when the day comes that you part with your pride and joy, what do you tell a prospective buyer when he queries you on the condition of your power plant?

Since maintenance intervals on boats cannot be based on miles operated, as they can in cars, the other reference you can use is hours of operation. While some engine panels are equipped with hour meters, they are often omitted on the smaller instrument panels of most auxiliary sailboats. The small engine needs an engine hour meter just as much as a big one. And of course, we can all do without the expense of replacing an engine, regardless of its size.

Hour meters are offered by many instrument manufactur-

The meter can be mounted in any convenient location, such as the navigation station below-decks.

ers; Datcon, Airguide, VDO, Teleflex, Medallion, and Stewart-Warner, to name a few. Retail prices range from about $30 to about $65 for a 12-volt, negative-ground hour meter needed for most small-boat installations.

The Hobbs Minimeter, model 15001-2, made by Stewart-Warner is one of the more popular units. It is water-resistant, so it can be installed in an existing cockpit-mounted instrument panel if there is room for it. However, since the hour meter is not an instrument you will refer to constantly while operating the engine, it can, of course, be installed in any convenient location above or below decks.

Templates are usually provided with the meters, indicating the diameter of the hole required to be cut for mounting. Most require a 2-inch-diameter hole, which can easily be cut with a hole saw in an electric drill. Three stainless steel screws secure the bezel in position. There is no distinction between positive and negative polarity with the Minimeter, and it is designed to work on systems between four and 40 volts DC.

One of the two electrical leads coming from the meter must be connected to part of the wiring system that is energized when the ignition key is in the "on" position. For convenience, the hot lead could be wired to the ignition switch, an electric fuel pump, or to one of the other engine instruments. The other lead is attached to a negative terminal. Obviously, to be accurate, the meter must operate only when the engine is running.

After you install the meter, check your owner's manual or contact the engine manufacturer for a copy of the recommended maintenance schedule for your particular engine. Each time a service is performed or an inspection is made, note the item in a maintenance log and indicate the engine hour reading. A detailed engine log will greatly enhance the resale value of your boat—not to mention your credibility as a conscientious skipper.

CONVERTING INTERIOR LIGHT FIXTURES FOR SAILING AT NIGHT

If you have ever done any night sailing, you understand the importance of having illumination belowdecks that allows you to maintain your night vision. Traditionally, this is done by painting the bulb in an existing overhead light with red nail polish, or by carrying a red-filtered flashlight. Some boats are also equipped with incandescent or fluorescent two-way fixtures, which allow you to choose between white or red light at the touch of a switch.

If your boat is equipped with overhead dome lights containing a single clear bulb, you may find that you can easily convert the fixtures for two-way operation. The two-way units contain a single-pole double-throw (SPDT) toggle switch, an additional bulb holder and bulb, and a red plastic bulb cover. These are items that are stocked by many electronics stores, or you can order them as replacement parts from Guest Corporation, a manufacturer of two-way cabin lighting fixtures.

The conversion itself is quite straightforward. The assemblies are first removed from the boat by taking off the lens and backing out the screws attaching the base of the light to the overhead. At this point, the fixtures will be hanging by their electrical conductors, which should be cut near the fixture. Next, remove the old single-pole toggle switch by unsoldering the leads, and insert the double-throw replacement. Then move an extra socket assembly and bulb around in the base to determine the best location. Drill a small hole in the base and mount the socket using a self-tapping screw or a pop rivet.

With the extra socket in place, both bulbs can now be wired

Most dome lights have room inside for both red and white bulbs.

to the switch. Attach one of the incoming leads, positive or negative, to the center lug of the switch and solder it securely. Next, attach two of the leads coming off the bulb sockets to the two remaining lugs of the switch. All remaining leads can be soldered or crimped together to complete the circuit. Now place the red cover over one bulb. Test the assembly before remounting it in the boat in case there are problems. Both bulbs should be off when the switch is in the center position, and each bulb should light independently of the other with the switch in the other positions. If the fixture passes bench testing, install the lens and splice it into the boat's wiring system with crimp-type butt connectors, which can also be soldered if you want a truly long-lasting connection.

*   *   *

For about $8 each and a little handiwork, your old dome lights can be updated to more functional night-vision fixtures. If you can't find the parts at a local electronics supplier, you can order them from Guest Corporation (Box 10130; West Hartford, CT 06110). The parts you will need per fixture are: one P11B04 toggle switch; one P11C09 bulb socket; and one P15201 bulb cover.

6

Cosmetic Improvements

HULL GRAPHICS: CHANGING YOUR BOAT'S LINES WITH A PAINTBRUSH

On the whole, we humans are an unreasonable lot. Architect Louis Sullivan's axiom, "form follows function" was not so much a rule for designers as it was social commentary: If we demand too much from our structures, we have no one but ourselves to blame for the way they turn out.

In the case of our boats, what do we expect when we demand standing headroom in a 30-footer, along with sleeping accommodations for six (including two separate cabins), a chart table, a big galley, and a comfortable saloon? We want something that looks like a Concordia yawl, but what we get is something that looks more like a cattle car. As boatowners, we are caught between the devil of our desires and the deep blue sea of physics and the limitations of our pocketbooks.

Ironically, we turn back to design—this time to graphic design—to bail us out of the jam we create with our desire for interior volume. In fact, using a few basic principles of graphic design, the often clunky and unflattering proportions of some of today's boats can be made to seem a little less high, a little less clunky, and a bit more flattering. All it takes is the judicious use of paint. A well thought-out cove stripe, boot-top, or graphic design can work wonders in improving a boat's appearance.

Before rushing out, paint brush in hand, to solve all your boat's aesthetic problems, do a little experimenting. We will outline a few general design principles shortly, but the first rule is: Looks count for everything. Every boat is unique; every boat poses its own challenge. What looks right on a boat with high freeboard and a flush deck might look out of place on a similar hull with a pilothouse.

The best approach is to try out several designs on paper first, before selecting one and committing it to the hull. Start with the sail plan, a brochure, or any drawing of the above-water profile of your boat. Even a photograph traced on white paper will work fine if it shows the boat dead abeam. Then make several copies of the drawing on which to try out your designs. Experiment with simple designs first, such as a wide boot-top on one profile, and a narrow cove stripe below the sheer on another. The simpler the design, the more effective it is likely to be and the easier it will be to execute. Keep experimenting, and hold onto the best designs. Try combining the drawings by holding them up to a strong light to test the effect of various combinations of boot stripes and sheer stripes. Even after you make a decision, give yourself at least several days to fully consider it.

Design Considerations

High, unbroken topsides make a boat look shorter. This effect is accentuated when the deck and deckhouse are the same color as the topsides. Any horizontal stripe that breaks up the uniformity of the topsides will make the boat seem longer and sleeker.

High topsides and a flush or nearly flush deck might benefit simply from a wide boot-top, either a single stripe or two or more narrower bands. On a boat with a tall cabin structure, a wide sheer stripe just below the toerail will lessen the boat's boxy appearance. Another technique that can help with a boxy deckhouse is to paint the coachroof a slightly darker shade than the sides of the house.

You do not have to limit yourself to horizontal stripes. Vertical stripes can make an area look shorter, which can help to bring hull components into proportion with one another. Sweeping the cove stripe down at its aft end can lend the aesthetics of a counter stern even to a boat with a boxy rear end.

The only line you cannot change is the waterline. Other than that, you add, accentuate, or delete any line depending on your taste. Nowhere is it written that all stripes on the topside must be parallel to each other or to some other line or hull feature. In fact, by making a cove stripe wider in the middle than at its ends, you can accentuate a boat's sheer. Likewise, making a boot-top wider at the bow and stern can also accentuate the sheer. When making these kinds of graphic additions, subtlety is important. The eye can be deceived by the clever use of graphics, but every sleight-of-hand has its limits.

Color is also an important consideration. Generally, darker colors make a boat look shorter and lower, while lighter colors make it look longer and higher. In addition to adding to the graceful appearance of a yacht, boot-tops have another function. They lie on the part of the hull most susceptible to dings and discoloration from floating debris, oil, algae, and so forth. Therefore, painting the boot-top a light color may work graphically, but may also require more frequent cleaning. Nevertheless, one of the most effective jobs of reducing the visual height of a massive topsides we have seen was achieved by painting a two-part boot-top six inches above the waterline on a boat that had a white topsides and white bottom paint. This created the illusion that the boat was floating well above her marks. It all goes to prove that all's fair in the topsides art game, as long as it works.

One option—a smart one in many cases—is to break up excessive freeboard with a rubbing strake, instead of a cove or sheer stripe. Not only do rubbing strakes save a lot of wear and tear on the topsides, but they are salty-looking, too, especially on boats of more traditional design.

To Paint Or Tape

The use of fancy colored tapes has been vogue in the auto industry for quite some time. Tape has advantages on boats, too. For one, it is fairly easy to find a wide variety of tapes from marine and auto-supply houses. They are not messy, and they are easy to change if you make a mistake. On the other hand, tape is not easy to apply and it cannot be repaired as easily as paint. If you have extensive graphics in mind, you might talk to an autobody shop about doing the work. Custom car painters also sometimes do boat painting and graphics, and frequently are more experienced at this type of work than boatyard painters.

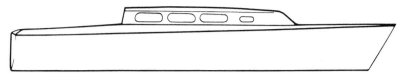

An unadorned hull appears dead in the water even when underway. Except for dinghies and workboats, all boats should have at least a simple boot-top.

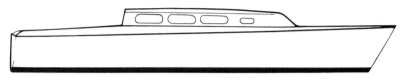

A boot-top makes a dramatic change in the appearance of the topsides. The stripe should be slightly wider at the bow and stern.

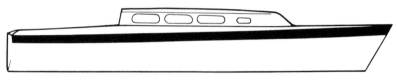

A bold sheer stripe can be effective for separating high deck structures from high topsides, particularly if the deckhouse and topsides are the same color.

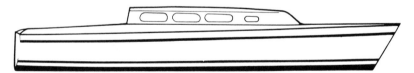

The combination of a cove stripe and a multipart boot-top helps to give a boat a long, low, racy look.

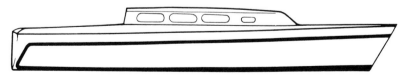

Incorporating a cove or sheer stripe into the boot-top at the after end can relieve the stern-heavy appearance of a boat with a broad, plumb transom.

Your marina or boatyard might know of people in your area who are professional boat graphics applicators, or you can check the classified section of boating publications for a shop that specializes in boat graphics. You might want an airbrushed design of some sort—some of them look very good—but this is the kind of work that must be done by an expert.

A Paint For All Seasons

The best paint to use for topsides graphics on a fiberglass boat is two-part polyurethane. It is expensive, especially if you need two or three different colors. It is also tricky to apply, although paint manufacturers are coming up with formulations these days that can be successfully applied with rollers and brushes (see Volume 3, *Maintenance and Repairs*, Chapter 4).

If your hull is getting on in years and the gelcoat is getting fairly chalky, it may be time to consider painting the entire hull before going to the trouble of applying an expensive graphics job. If your gelcoat is tired, use a less expensive alkyd-type paint for your graphics until the hull is refinished. Not only would it be a waste of money to use expensive paint for what will amount to temporary graphics, but it will add to the time necessary to prepare the hull for refinishing. And, of course, a shiny new cove stripe or boot-top would look incongruous on an otherwise chalky-looking hull.

CARVE A CUSTOM NAMEBOARD

For saltiness and elegance, few things beat a hand-carved name-board gracing the stern of a proper yacht. However, having one made is expensive, for the artist must earn a fair wage and much time is involved.

The alternative, of course, is to carve your own nameboard. It is not nearly as difficult as you might imagine, but patience and care are required. Here's how to do it step by step.

First plan and design the board. The size and shape are largely determined by your yacht's transom. About 75 percent of the transom width is a good rule of thumb for the overall length of the board, with the width in proportion to the length. The top

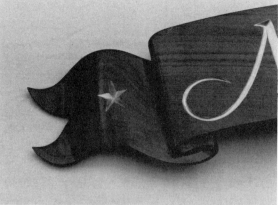

The wings of the nameboard can be carved to achieve a "windblown" effect. Note how the wing appears to fold back behind the main board.

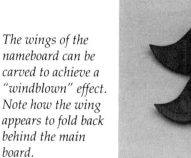

and bottom edges of the board should follow the sheer line of the transom. The ribbon style is traditional for a stern nameboard.

After developing the overall design of the nameboard, take the time to draw it out full-size on posterboard or cardboard. This step will allow you to get an "artist's feel" for the overall design while changes can still be made with an eraser.

We would not use any other wood but teak for a nameboard. Teak is a heavy, dense wood with uniform grain. It resists splintering very well, and cuts rather easily for a hardwood. Teak is expensive, but well worth it for a project like this, where the time invested greatly outweighs the cost of the materials. Few lumberyards carry teak, but larger cities usually have at least one hardwood lumber supplier, or you can order teak through the mail from one of the many marine lumber dealers. They will also mill the stock to your order for a reasonable additional charge. You may want to buy a little extra to use to practice carving one or two letters.

The next step is to make your nameboard. For more realism and a three dimensional look, cut the "wings" separately and glue them with epoxy to the back of the main part of the nameboard. For even more realism, after gluing, carve the wings to get a "blowing in the wind" look. This is reasonably easy to do, but use extra thought and care when carving the detail which shows the ribbon curling back behind the main nameboard.

If your transom is fairly flat, the wings will raise the name-

This board was laminated to fit the curvature of the transom. The letters are being adjusted until the letter spacing appears right.

board off the transom and make it unnecessary to bend the board. However, if you must bend your board, the best way to do it is by lamination.

Begin by measuring the curvature of your boat's transom. Have a friend hold a piece of cardboard on edge against the transom. Then, hold a compass so that the point leg rides against the transom and the pencil leg scribes the curve of the transom on the cardboard. Now cut the cardboard on the line you scribed.

From 1/4-inch teak stock, cut three identical boards, each a little longer and wider than the main part of the nameboard. From scrap wood, cut three blocks of wood, each as long as your boards are wide. One should be as thick as the center of the bent board will be high. The other two should be as thick as the bent board will be high at the midpoints between the center and the ends of the board. Nail these three blocks to a 2x10 plank which is a little longer than your nameboard. Space the blocks so that they will force a curve in your laminations which is identical to your cardboard template.

Now try a dry run. Two large C-clamps should be sufficient to bend your laminations. Be sure to pad your clamps with short

1x2s to keep your laminations from cupping or cracking. If everything goes well, you are ready to glue.

We recommend epoxy glue because it will fill minor gaps without any loss in strength and it does not require that the laminate be under pressure throughout. After mixing, brush or roll unthickened epoxy on all surfaces to be glued. Now add a thickener (sanding dust or colodial silica) to your remaining mixed epoxy—just enough to keep the epoxy from running. Spread a liberal amount of the thickened epoxy on the glue side of the two outside laminations. Now stack your laminations on your bending blocks and clamp. It helps to have an assistant because the boards tend to slip and slide when you take up on the clamps. If after clamping, there are any significant gaps in your glue lines, use smaller C-clamps and pads to squeeze the boards together. Do not use unnecessary pressure or you will starve the lamination of glue. And don't forget to protect your clamp pads with waxed paper, so they will not become glued to the board.

After the epoxy has cured overnight, take the clamps off, cut the board to shape, and attach and carve the wings as described above. Sand the entire board first with 80-grit paper until it is free of tool marks, and then sand once again with 120 or 150 grit.

Letter style is a matter of personal taste. Plain block letters are easier to draw and carve. Most libraries have books containing alphabets of various letter styles. There are also many other sources to select from. For instance, the letter style could be taken from a magazine or an artist's type catalog.

After selecting the letter style, carefully draw each letter of your boat's name on index cards. A draftsman's dividers will help keep the letters to scale. For example, if the letters are to be five times the height of the sample, then every dimension of the sample can be projected full size simply by "walking" the dividers five steps.

Use small, sharp scissors to cut out the letters. For letters that occur more than once in your yacht's name, make duplicates by tracing the cut-out letters on another card. Use a sharp pencil to guard against making the duplicates larger than the originals.

Now, on your nameboard draw a line where the bottom of your letters will rest. Then place your cut-out letters on the board. The spaces between the letters should not be a set meas-

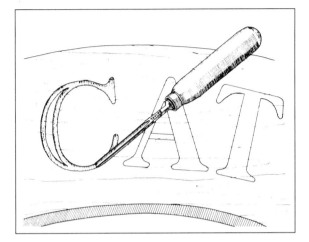

*Give careful atten-
tion to the width
and style of the
letters before buy-
ing tools. This
3/16-inch gouge is
perfect for carving
letters with
rounded grooves.*

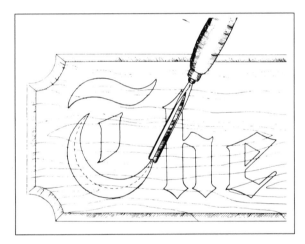

*For making in-
cised or V-shaped
grooves, begin the
cut with a V-
gouge by cutting
parallel to the
outline of the
letter.*

urement. Rather, the shape of the letter and that of the one next to it determines the amount of "negative space" left in between. Again, use your "artist's eye."

Having laid out the letters as best you can, walk away and come back and look again. View the board from different distances and angles. When fully satisfied, very carefully trace the outline of each letter on the board. Use a fine-tip, ball-point pen. Unlike pencil lines, ink will not rub away as you work.

Buy high-quality carving tools (gouges and skews). It is not necessary to buy a complete set; buy only what you will need for this project. Tool requirements will depend upon the letter style

For carving fine details, it is better to push the gouge than to tap it with the mallet. Guide the tool with one hand while pushing gently with the other.

and whether the cuts are round or V-shaped. In any case, you will need two or three different size gouges and a small to medium-size skew. For V-shaped cuts, you will also need a V-gouge. In addition, you will also need a woodcarver's mallet; a carpenter's claw hammer simply will not do.

Inspect your new tools. They must be razor sharp and kept that way. Teak is more abrasive than most woods, so frequent resharpening is required. When sharpening, be careful not to destroy the original shapes and angles of your tools.

If this is your first carving experience, practice one or two letters on a piece of scrap teak. This will develop tool-handling confidence, help develop carving techniques, and give you a good feel for the grain performance.

In describing carving techniques, we will deal first with the round-track letter, and then with the V-bottom or "incised" letter, as used for *Magnolia*. Of course, many other styles exist, but the basic carving techniques for the round and incised letters can be applied to all other variations.

For rounded letters, begin with a gouge equal in width to the narrow lines in each letter. First, cut the entire outline of the letters, including the wide parts, using this narrow gouge. Then remove the material in the center of the wide parts by using a wider gouge. The size gouge used will, of course, depend upon the size of the letters

The direction of cut is parallel to the outline of the letter. Place the gouge on the wood so that when you reach the desired depth, the cutting edge of the gouge will be just reaching the outline of the letter, or slightly inside. Fine trimming exactly to the line can be done later. Clamp the board firmly to your workbench, and use the mallet to power the gouge with a light tap, tap, tap. If you are patient, use the mallet with a little finesse, and watch the grain direction, there is little chance of making a slip that will destroy your work.

In some situations, it will be more convenient to push the gouge by hand. To avoid potentially dangerous slipping always use both hands, one to guide the gouge and the other to push with. And again, be sure the gouge is very sharp in order to avoid unnecessary pressure that will make the tool hard to control.

An entirely different technique is used for "V" or incised letters. The skew is the fundamental tool for the straight portions of the letters. The direction of cut is perpendicular to the outline of the letter and the skew is held at an angle of approximately 45 degrees to the surface of the board. Make the first cuts just slightly to either side of the imaginary line which would be the bottom of the groove when it is completed. Gradually work out until reaching the edge of the outline of the letter.

For the final cut, which is made at the outline, exercise great care in placing the skew perfectly before giving it the first strike with the mallet. The cutting edge of the skew must be exactly on the line, otherwise you will not get a continuously smooth surface from one cut to the next. For this reason it is also important to cut at the same angle from both sides so that the line formed by the "V" is straight and in the center of the letter.

When cutting the curved and pointed portions of letters, the V-gouge is useful. Place it just inside the starting point. Begin the cut by holding the gouge at less of an angle than you will on the final cut. Take out a little material at a time and gradually

The letter style used for Magnolia *is an example of "V" or incised style letters.This particular type style is an amalgam of styles found in* The Practical Guide to Lettering & Applied Calligraphy *by Rosemary Sassoon (Thames and Hudson, Inc.; New York, NY).*

increase the angle of the gouge until you have removed just the amount of material necessary.

In wider, curved portions of letters, such as in an old English "T", the V-gouge will not cut to full width, but it is a good tool to begin with. When you have cut as far as possible with the V-gouge, finish up with a rounded gouge and skew. Use the gouge on the outside edge of the curve, and cut perpendicular to the outline, letting the curved cutting edge of the gouge follow the curvature of the letter. On the inside edge of the curve, use the skew, again cutting perpendicular to the outline of the letter. Cut a little at a time to avoid splitting the wood. Alternate cutting with the gouge and skew until reaching the outline. Again, remember to maintain a constant angle of cut from both sides to ensure the V-bottom forms a line exactly between the outlines.

It is impossible to detail every carving technique. No set rules exist with regard to tools and techniques for achieving a certain cut. As you work, you will discover the best tools and techniques. And, although we don't use one, there is no reason why a router can't be used for rough cutting, with hand tools used for finishing up. If you use a router, however, be extremely careful; they tend to produce inexact cuts when used freehand.

Keep making practice letters until you are successful. There is no point in moving to the actual nameboard until you have fully mastered the carving techniques. (Hopefully, at this point you won't decide to rename your yacht something with only three or four letters.) Each letter does take considerable time; but after each is successfully carved, you will feel more and more pride in the project.

Finish each letter as carefully as possible with carving tools, so that very little sanding is required. When sanding, use care to avoid rounding edges that should remain sharp. To do so would destroy the precise, crisp outline of the letters.

After sanding the board, the letters should be colored. Gold is the traditional color. Gold enamel looks good at first, but it tarnishes quickly. Although it is expensive, gold leaf is the best treatment. If you want to do it yourself, your library probably has books describing gilding techniques, or you can employ a local sign painter to apply the gold leaf.

If you are going to paint your letters, don't worry about applying the paint perfectly. After it dries, sand the face of the board with your paper wrapped tightly around a wooden sanding block. You will sand away any paint which has strayed outside the letters.

The finish you apply to your nameboard will depend upon what you do to the other wood trim on your yacht. If you use oil on your other teak, oil the board; if you varnish, varnish the board. If you are going to apply gold leaf, apply two or three coats of varnish before leafing. First scrub the board thoroughly with acetone to remove surface oils. Then apply the first coat with the varnish coat thinned by twenty-five percent so that it penetrates the pores of the wood well. The remaining coats can be put on unthinned. Sand lightly between coats and sand the last coat over before applying the sizing for the gold leaf. After gold leafing, apply three or four more coats of varnish.

The final step is to mount your new nameboard on the stern of your yacht. ...No need to blush when you tell the fellow in the next slip where your nameboard came from. That sense of pride is richly deserved.

Index